Sep

How the
Chinese
Created
CANADA

How the
Chinese
Created
CANADA

ADRIAN MA

DRAGON
HILL

© 2010 by Dragon Hill Publishing Ltd.
First printed in 2010 10 9 8 7 6 5 4 3 2 1
Printed in Canada

The Publisher: Dragon Hill Publishing Ltd.

Library and Archives Canada Cataloguing in Publication

Ma, Adrian, 1983–
    How the Chinese created Canada / Adrian Ma.
Includes bibliographical references.

ISBN 978-1-896124-19-3
    1. Chinese Canadians—History. 2. Chinese—Canada—History.
3. Canada—Civilization—Chinese influences. I. Title.

FC106.C5M3   2009 971'.004951   C2009-900412-7

Project Director: Gary Whyte
Project Editor: Kathy van Denderen
Cover Image: Courtesy of © iStockphoto | Leonsbox
Photo Credits: Every effort has been made to accurately credit the sources of the images. Any errors or omissions should be directed to the publisher for changes in future editions. Glenbow Museum (p. 40, NA-3740-29; p. 54, NA-103-30; p. 131, NA-1497-9; p. 168, ND-2-109; p. 205, PA-2453-378; p. 218, ND-3-5957); Library and Archives Canada (p. 32, 3192437, p. 118, 3192435; p. 119, 3630098).

We acknowledge the support of the Alberta Foundation for the Arts for our publishing program.

CONTENTS

DEDICATION

To my loving parents, Andrew and Rebecca,
for giving me the two greatest gifts I have ever
received—Chinese blood and a Canadian heart.

Thanks, eh.

Acknowledgements

Special thanks to everyone at Dragon Hill for their support and assistance. My eternal gratitude also goes out to editor Kathy van Denderen.

To Matthew Purdy and Emma Lashbrook—thanks for the use of your library cards. I hope this makes us even on the overdue charges. Sorry 'bout that.

My best to Mark Bieksa, Dan Bobzener, Jay Wynne, Jeff Rochwerg, Heather Padgett, Carly Beath, Ryerson Masters of Journalism Class of 2009 and many other friends for their constant encouragement.

Merci beaucoup to the lovely Elizabeth Arbour and her wonderful family for their graciousness and somewhat inexplicable (but much appreciated) confidence in me.

All my love to my family—Mom, Dad, Amanda and Chris.

Thanks to Wayson Choy, Norman Kwong, Paul Yee, Peter Li, David Lai, Adrienne Clarkson and countless others for their unique contributions to Chinese Canadian culture and history.

And, finally, thanks to the many Chinese who first led the way in Canada. This book can only scratch the surface of your amazing narrative. We Canadians are all in your debt.

Do jeh saai ("thank you so much," in Cantonese).

INTRODUCTION

This book, as you have no doubt noticed, is entitled *How the Chinese Created Canada*. Trust me, it's a grand tale indeed. It has everything: exotic locales, dangerous journeys across oceans, inspiring characters, heartbreaking moments and the eventual triumph of right over wrong. It's a true underdog story, based on actual events. And there's also some kung fu. Who doesn't love kung fu?

But before I continue on with this story, I'd like to provide a little background on this book and its author. I agree with Ralph Waldo Emerson when he said, "there is properly no history, only biography." If you, kind reader, would permit me a moment of navel-gazing self-indulgence, I'd like to begin with the history of my own parents' journey to Canada in a section I'd like to call "How Canada Created My Chinese Family."

My parents were born and raised on Hong Kong Island, a beautiful, bustling port city on the South China Sea. They both arrived in Canada as students during the early 1970s, as it was popular back then for Chinese parents to send their kids to schools overseas (if they could afford it) to learn English.

My father, Andrew, ended up studying at St. Michaels University School in Victoria, British Columbia, a historic private boarding school that boasts several notable alumni, including former prime minister Paul Martin, journalist and former senator Laurier LaPierre and shaggy-haired basketball superstar Steve Nash. After graduating, my father headed to Ontario, where he attended Confederation College in Thunder Bay and then the University of Waterloo.

My mother, Rebecca, came to Toronto with her family to finish high school and then went to Mohawk College in Hamilton, Ontario. My parents met through mutual acquaintances, fell in love, married and decided to raise a family in Canada instead of returning to Hong Kong. For quite some time, I thought this was the magnitude of their history, at least before my birth in 1983.

My mother and father raised me and my younger sister, Amanda, in a lovely three-bedroom, two-car-garage home in the leafy suburb of Ancaster, near Hamilton. It's a place that resembles many of the other middle-class bedroom communities in southern Ontario—quiet, predominately white, with one Canadian Tire and one movie theatre.

I didn't think much of being Chinese back then. We spoke a mix of Chinese and English at home (especially English when I was in trouble—to make sure I really understood the gravity of the situation), but my life was no different than those of my childhood friends, whose families had come from Europe to Canada a few generations before mine.

I went to school, preferred academics instead of athletics, read Gordon Korman books, watched *Power Rangers* and played Nintendo with my friends. I also loved hanging out in my basement, a large, perpetually cluttered dark refuge where I could let my imagination run wild. I'd occasionally construct a primitive suit of armour from plastic garbage bags, grab a flashlight and hunt for ghosts in the deep recesses near the furnace. My best friend, Matt, and I would often pretend we were superheroes and engage in epic battles on the two battered couches that sat in our basement. Other times, I'd just rummage through the stuff my parents had amassed over the years.

There was one small room in the basement where we kept old things in. Items such as school textbooks, busted record players and worn-out suitcases. There were also photos on the wall, mostly of my mother when she was in her early 20s. I remember thinking how pretty she looked in those photos, like a Chinese version of Kate Jackson from *Charlie's Angels* (their haircuts were kind of similar).

But another photo always stuck with me: a large, black-and-white one of my mom and an older Chinese gentleman who was shaking hands with a dapper, grey-haired white man with a large grin. They were all wearing fancy clothes. I assumed it was some party, maybe a wedding, and never bothered to ask about it.

Years later, I was in seventh-grade history class reading about The Canada Act of 1982 in a textbook. This important act made Canada a fully sovereign state and contained the Charter of Rights and Freedoms, which guarantees Canadians several rights, including religious freedom, minority language tolerance and free speech. I learned it was a difficult negotiation, spearheaded by the prime minister at the time, Pierre Trudeau. My eyes were drawn to a black-and-white photo of Mr. Trudeau sitting with Queen Elizabeth II as she signed the document.

And there he was. The grey-haired white man with the large grin. The man from the photo with my mom! My mom had shaken hands with Canada's philosopher king? The guy who loved to canoe? When I got home that night, I asked my mom about it immediately. Yes, she had met Trudeau, she told me. Then she explained to me how she came to Canada.

My mother's oldest brother was the first of her family to gain permanent residency in Canada, and he was able to sponsor their parents and younger siblings to come here as well. After finishing school, my mother's student visa was no longer valid, and she was too old to be considered a dependent child. Her family was able to stay in Canada, but she would have to return to Hong Kong and apply for entrance from there.

My mom was put in touch with a Chinese lawyer who helped her with her application. One night, she said, the lawyer called and told her Trudeau was coming to a fund-raising event in Toronto, and they should try to meet him. She dressed up, went to the event and met the prime minister. While they were chatting, the lawyer handed someone in Trudeau's entourage a letter detailing my mom's immigration case. She didn't know exactly what happened, but the administrative hurdles she had been facing went away. Within a few weeks, she was informed she was allowed to stay in Canada with her family.

That little anecdote grew into something of mythological proportion in my mind. My mom is unsure of the facts because the event happened over 30 years ago when she was new and unfamiliar with this country. That she met Trudeau is true, and that her lawyer friend presented his staff with a letter appealing her case is also true. That Trudeau *himself* had anything to do with bringing her to Canada (and consequently, giving my parents the chance to meet) is unknown and highly unlikely. Still, if I ever found myself in a situation like Michael J. Fox in *Back to the Future* (you know, the scene where he has to get his parents to kiss at the Enchantment Under the Sea dance or else he'd never exist), I'd sure as heck travel back in time to make sure my mom got to that Liberal Party event.

In a way, though, Trudeau did have a hand in bringing my parents together. It was Trudeau who sparked a revolution in Canadian culture by ushering in the era of multiculturalism. His government updated antiquated immigration policies to be more inclusive, compassionate and sympathetic to refugees and divided families. It was a significant departure from Canada's previous immigration policies that had often denied people entrance into the country on racial and ideological grounds.

Ever since my Trudeau epiphany, I became much more aware of the sometimes sad but inspiring history of the Chinese in Canada. To me, my parents were trailblazers in their own right —leaving Hong Kong and trying to make a life for themselves in a land where they spoke little English and had few friends. They made it. They worked hard to establish a textile business that employed hundreds of Canadians. But as I grew up, I learned that, in the same way that I owe a debt of gratitude to my parents for their courage and perseverance, they, too, owe the Chinese who came before them. And you know what? So do Canadians of every stripe.

One of Canada's most beautiful qualities and greatest strengths is the diversity of its people. From the very beginning, people of many different ethnicities have contributed to the growth and development of this country.

We're here today because of their toil, their sacrifice, their drive and their enduring spirit.

You may not consider the Chinese one of Canada's founding heritages, but their contribution to this country is just as immeasurable as the legacies of the French, the Scottish, the English and, of course, the First Nations. Canada, as we know it today, would not exist if it weren't for those brave Chinese pioneers who helped to settle the frontier West of the late 19th century, build the nation's railway and step into the difficult, backbreaking jobs few others wanted. Industries desperate for labour welcomed them with open arms, then shunned them after the work was done.

The Chinese people overcame intense racism—from the general public and from our own government that in 1885 slapped a head tax on Chinese immigrants, a discriminatory political act never before seen in Canadian history and never seen since. Chinese immigrants were told they didn't belong, but they stayed and made homes here regardless. Some of their children fought for this country in World War II. Many Canadian-born Chinese studied hard and qualified for good jobs.

Since the late 20th century, the Chinese have proven to be invaluable to Canada as a growing, entrepreneurial class, contributing global business connections, ideas and innovations, and promoting a rich culture of art, cuisine and spirituality that has become mainstream. Canada's ethnic Chinese form the country's second largest visible minority group, accounting for almost four percent of the total population. This is an amazing development considering that the Canadian government actually banned most Chinese immigration from 1923 until after World War II. And with China's emergence as a global economic and political superpower, Chinese

Canadians will play an important role as Canada's engagement with this Asian giant strengthens.

It has been a spectacular rise for a people who were once given "a Chinaman's chance" to survive. But survive they did. And this book aims to explain how they managed to do so.

CHAPTER ONE

THE DRAGON PEOPLE

People of Chinese heritage around the world often refer to themselves as "descendants of the dragon," and they do so proudly. The mythical Chinese dragon—sleek, serpentine and whiskered, unlike the winged, fire-breathing behemoths depicted in Western medieval culture and popularized by fantasy game nerds—holds an esteemed place in Chinese history. Folk tales about dragons and symbols shaped in its image are as old as Chinese culture itself—about 5000 years, according to most estimates.

In ancient China, dragons were respected for their wisdom, admired for their strength, praised for their graciousness and beloved as guardian angels of the land. They had magical powers that were capable of great destruction, but dragons were always benevolent in their use. The ancient Chinese believed dragons controlled the rain, rivers and seas—an early explanation for environmental changes in the pre-scientific age. In short, they were like loyal guard dogs that had the added bonus of blessing you with crops, financial prosperity and even fertility. It's no wonder dragons were adopted as symbols of China's imperial emperors.

The icon of the dragon remains central to Chinese ethnic identity, even though many supposed descendants of the dragon now reside in the land of polar bears, beavers and Wiarton Willie—the Ontario groundhog that predicts when spring is coming. But despite a common mythological ancestor, the Chinese have a lot less in common than many people assume.

Before we explore the incredible story of how the dragon people became such an integral part of the Canadian population, I'd like to clarify some of the terms and concepts used throughout this book. Without some historical and cultural context (or at least, a reasonable stab at providing it), navigating the deep waters of Chinese Canadian history can be somewhat murky.

First, the definition of "Chinese" can be a complicated issue, especially regarding ethnic identity. Everyone is familiar with the common stereotype that says it's hard to tell Asian people apart, and, as a person of Chinese ancestry, I can definitely see the point. After all, there's only so much aesthetic variation when, for the most part, every Chinese person is born with black hair and brown eyes. Although Chinese people may all look similar to some, there are key ethnic distinctions to consider.

China is home to 56 ethnic groups (that are officially recognized by the People's Republic of China, anyway), including the Han, the Zhuang, the Manchu, the Hui and the Uyghur. Although all these groups originate within the boundaries of today's China, many speak their own dialects and maintain their own unique traditions and customs.

The Han Chinese is by far the largest ethnic group, accounting for more than 90 percent of all people in China and approximately 20 percent of the world's total population. So when you see iconic symbols of mainstream Chinese culture—such as lantern festivals, dragon boat races, wonton noodle soup, Jackie Chan and so on—you're more than likely looking at a slice of Han Chinese culture.

But the minority groups are also important to consider. They constitute less than 10 percent of China's population of 1.4 billion, but that's still nearly 140 million people. The Zhuang, for example, are China's leading ethnic minority, with over 16 million people—only about one percent of China's population but nearly half of Canada's total population!

Ethnic equality in China has a long, complex history and continues to be at the root of some sensitive political issues today. Throughout the centuries, there have been conflicts between the Han Chinese (and by extension, the Han-controlled government) and many of the other groups (notably the Tibetans and Uyghur people) over religious rights, language, economic opportunity, cultural assimilation and political autonomy. However, there are examples of relatively successful integration. The Islam-practising Hui, at 10 million strong and scattered throughout the country, are often cited as an ethnic group that co-exists with the central government. But ethnic tensions do tend to simmer, sometimes resulting in violent protests and deadly clashes.

It's important to acknowledge that China is a multi-ethnic nation and that the individual cultures should be respected. However, for the purposes of this book, when I refer to the Chinese, I'm referring largely to the Han Chinese. The overwhelming majority of Chinese immigrants to this country are Han Chinese, and this is the brand of culture we Canadians understand and accept as Chinese.

Ethnic make-up aside (as if the identity issues weren't confusing enough), Chinese people often differentiate themselves based on whether or not they're from the People's Republic of China (PRC; includes mainland and Hong Kong, which, along with Macau, is considered to be a special administrative region). Although people in mainland China, Hong Kong and Taiwan (Republic of China, ROC, which includes some minor islands as well) may all consider themselves Chinese, these regions have each developed unique distinctions, especially when it comes to cuisine, popular culture (such as movies and music), political identity (democracy or communism) and language.

Historically, Taiwan and Hong Kong were ceded by China following defeats in war (to the Japanese and British, respectively). They've since been released by their colonizers—Taiwan in 1945, Hong Kong in 1997—but both societies developed separate, sovereign identities and have since operated with some political autonomy. The PRC, for its part, maintains there is only one China, which includes Taiwan and Hong Kong. This position has left Taiwan and Hong Kong in political limbo, as many Taiwanese desire to remain independent from China, and Hong Kong has a constitution that guarantees universal suffrage some day.

Talk to many Taiwanese or Hong Kongers and they'd argue that while ethnically they're all Chinese, they're all different people culturally and socially. In this book, I refer to "Chinese" as a general term for anyone from these regions, but I do my best to indicate where certain traditions and practices came from—the mainland, Hong Kong or Taiwan and so forth.

The Chinese language is something I should also touch upon. As many readers may already know, Chinese is not merely one particular language but is a family of hundreds of regional dialects: 400 of them in total! And it's not the same as the difference between Parisian French and Québécois French. Although the Chinese share essentially the same writing system (consisting of over 47,000 characters, of which a person must learn 3–4000 in order to be considered literate), each province, town, city and even village may utilize its own unique patois. There are grammatical similarities, but the differences in pronunciation, accent and vernacular can be vastly diverse. Two Chinese people speaking different dialects of Chinese might not be able to understand each other.

The two most commonly spoken dialects of Chinese are Mandarin, the primary language in mainland China, and Cantonese, mostly spoken by the natives of Guangdong on the mainland and the island regions of Hong Kong and Macau. Some of the other more widely spoken regional dialects include Shanghainese, Sichuanese, Hunanese and, of course, Taiwanese.

Mandarin, or Putonghua, is China's official language and is spoken by most people in the country, making it the most commonly used language in the entire world. Using the Beijing dialect as a model, Mandarin was promoted as a solution to the communication issues resulting from so many regional dialects. Chinese officials had tried to establish a national language as early as the 18th century but had little success. When the PRC formed in 1949, they quickly established Mandarin as the nation's common language. Today, nearly all schools in China and Taiwan teach in Mandarin. China's recent economic rise has now made learning Mandarin increasingly popular. According to *The New York Times*, nearly 100,000 foreigners went to China to study Mandarin in 2006, more than double the number five years earlier. In total, nearly 900 million people speak Mandarin around the world, more than twice as many as those who speak English.

Although not nearly as widely used as Mandarin, Cantonese-style dialects were far more common in North America prior to the 21st century. This is because the majority of early Chinese immigrants came from the region of Guangdong in Southern China. Indeed, of the 5056 Chinese in British Columbia during the early 1880s who made donations to the Chinese Consolidated Benevolent Association, nearly two-thirds originated from the four Guangdong counties of Taishan, Kaiping, Xinhui and Enping. If you had visited a Chinatown in North America between 1848 and 1999, you'd very likely have heard a Guangdong dialect such as Taishanese, which sounds similar to Cantonese. It has only been in the last decade or so that mainland China has overtaken Hong Kong in immigration to Canada.

Just for fun, here's an example of the differences between English, Mandarin and Cantonese:

English: "I am Chinese."

Mandarin: "*Wo shi Chongwen-ren.*"

Cantonese: "*Ngoh hai Jung Gwok-yun.*"

And there remains the sometimes sticky issue of what to call Chinese people who were born or live outside of China. In 2006, more than 1.3 million people of Chinese ethnicity were living in Canada, according to Statistics Canada. Of those Chinese, about 25 percent were born in Canada; the other 75 percent were immigrants. Some Chinese in Canada prefer to be referred to as "Chinese," while others, more often the Canadian-born ones, think of themselves as "Canadian." In order to simplify things for this book, whenever I use the term "Chinese Canadian,"

I'm referring to people of Chinese heritage who were born in Canada or immigrated here.

The differences in languages and political identity are just the beginning. There is amazing variation within Chinese culture when it comes to cuisine, folk music, festivals, spiritual practices and art. And many of these unique, regional elements of Chinese culture have become incredibly popular in the West, from Taiwanese bubble tea to Hong Kong–style action cinema.

But when the Chinese first set foot in Canada, it didn't matter whether they spoke Cantonese, Taishanese or Mandarin, or whether they considered themselves to be from China. All Chinese were foreigners, and they were never expected to stay. But stay they did.

Despite the diversity among early Chinese immigrants, many shared similar values that are still associated with Chinese culture to this day. It was these values that helped them survive in a foreign place. Family is the most important pillar of Chinese society. In China, land and wealth were passed down from generation to generation, so it was important for adult Chinese to have children—a lot of them. Families with the same surname (such as Lee, Ma, Chan) belonged to a clan, a mass collective that pooled their resources and money to build necessities such as roads and schools in their villages.

When Chinese workers travelled to North America, they sent money back to their clan villages. Clan affiliations would play a very significant role in Canada, as many of the first Chinese Canadian organizations evolved from different surname groups. Sticking together was the only the way the Chinese could overcome the challenges that lay ahead for them in "Gold Mountain."

Chapter Two

Early Adventures and Gold Mountain

We had been wed for only a few nights;
Then you left me for Gold Mountain.
For twenty long years you haven't returned.
For this, I embrace only resentment in my bedroom.
—Old Chinese poem

The Chinese arrived in Canada in waves. Interestingly enough, some historians believe the Chinese were the first non-Natives to set foot in North America. Some historical evidence suggests that a man named Hui Shen led a small contingent of Buddhist monks to North America in 459 CE, landing somewhere off the coast of Mexico and then travelling north to California and British Columbia. Ancient Chinese coins and a stone anchor were discovered off the California coast. After returning to China in 499 CE., Hui Shen wrote a document detailing the exploits of his trip, which included rudimentary maps, descriptions of the Natives (he was decidedly snobby) and references to plants that modern historians believe were American aloe. If indeed Hui Shen made the 11,000-kilometre journey to North America, then he beat European explorer Christopher Columbus by more than 1000 years. Impressive if it's true, not that the Chinese tend to brag.

What's definitely true is that the Chinese set foot in British Columbia in 1788. An ex-Royal Navy captain-turned-merchant named John Meares decided to set up a fur-trading post on the west coast of what is now Canada. Meares had been trading in Asia and entered into a partnership with a Portuguese merchant while in Macau, the island near Hong Kong that had been a Portuguese colony since the 16th century. From Macau, Meares assembled the crew he would take to Canada, which included about 50 Chinese shipbuilders, metalworkers, carpenters and sailors.

That group eventually found itself at Friendly Cove on Nootka Sound, on the west side of Vancouver Island. There, the Chinese craftsmen got to work, building a two-storey fort, a residence, a shipyard and a schooner, which was a significant event because it was the first ship (in contrast to the dugout canoes of the First Nations) ever built on the Pacific Northwest coast. Later in 1788, Meares set sail for the Queen Charlotte Islands with a crew made up of Chinese and British. Some of the Chinese voyagers stayed behind, though, and are believed to have married into the local Native communities. The fate of these early Chinese colonists is unclear, but reports over the next 45 years suggested the Chinese workers mixed in well with the local society, married Native women, made homes and lived out the rest of their days in the New World.

The first major group of immigrants from China came about a century later. They came looking for riches but found something else entirely: a new home. In the late 1840s, news reverberated around the world that gold had been struck on the west coast of the United States. Soon, thousands of enterprising workers from Latin American, European and Asian nations crossed the ocean and joined the locals, descending into caves or panning California's streams for the precious metal.

A small cluster of Chinese men arrived at California's ports eager to join the hunt. How strange, frightening and wondrous it must have been for them. In this new land, warm with sunshine, they could literally fish wealth out of the cool waters or pull it from cave walls. If they sifted through enough stones, collected enough fistfuls of the bright yellow bounty, they could return to their villages prosperous and respected.

Despite the myriad dangers involved with such an endeavour (beginning with a two-month ocean voyage on a cramped, leaky boat), optimism surrounded this *Gam Saan* ("Gold Mountain"). After all, whatever risks they'd face in this new continent couldn't have been much more dangerous than remaining in China at the time.

Like many European immigrants before them, the Chinese arrived on North American shores to escape famine and to seek out better economic opportunities. For centuries, the Chinese empire's power and stature within the international community had been growing, but China had descended into disarray a few decades before the gold rush in the West.

China's Rise and Fall

China's Ming Dynasty rulers (1368–1644) had always been concerned about Western imperialism and influence, so they pursued isolationist policies, limiting foreign trade within the country. The Qing Dynasty (1644–1911) that followed had the same attitude and continued to intensely regulate foreign trade and activity.

In the early 17th century, after the British attempted to expand trade in several northern Chinese ports, the empire decreed all foreign trade would be conducted from one location: the port of Canton, capital city of the Guangdong province in the south. Canton (now known as Guangzhou) quickly became the busiest, most bustling trading centre in the Chinese empire. Crates of spices, tea and silk were constantly loaded onto ships waiting to sail back to Europe. In return, Western traders imported two primary items: silver bullion and opium, the painkilling narcotic derived from poppy plants grown in British-controlled India.

The Canton trading system, as it came to be known, presented some benefits to all parties involved. For China, it provided a measure of control, and, for the British and the rest of the foreign countries, it allowed them a foot in the door of the immense Chinese market. But foreign merchants soon grew unhappy with the numerous regulations set in place by the Qing authorities. While in China, foreigners were often slapped with arbitrary fees and fines levied by officials and were subject to Chinese law that presumed the accused were guilty until proven innocent. Unjust imprisonment and torture weren't uncommon. China also refused to allow any foreign warships, or women for that matter, into the area.

But what really raised the foreigners' hackles was the huge trade imbalance that eventually emerged. The British were absolutely hooked on tea and bought millions of kilograms of the Chinese-grown leaves every year. But the Chinese had no real interest in European products, except for precious metals, which were extremely expensive to ship over to China.

So part of the new British business plan was to start flooding China with opium, which Chinese merchants paid for with the silver bullion they also bought from English merchants. Opium had been used for medicinal purposes in China since around the 13th century, but the British now marketed it as a recreational, smokable drug (imagine how Don Draper and company would tackle *that* ad campaign on the TV show *Mad Men*).

Chinese officials desperately tried to suppress the drug trade, but corrupt port authorities and opportunistic Chinese merchants ignored these efforts. By 1836, over 1800 tons of opium had been smuggled into China. It's estimated that one out of every eight citizens became a habitual user. The trade advantage China once held had been reversed, and illegal opium was now bleeding China dry of wealth and was sickening its society.

The Chinese appealed to British officials to stop supplying the drug and circumventing prohibition laws, but the pleas fell upon deaf ears. China got fed up. In 1839, in a bold, aggressive move, Chinese authorities seized over 20,000 chests of opium from Canton storage houses and flushed them into the sea. The British merchants were furious and appealed to their government. England cried foul. Destroying the drugs sparked the powder keg that led to the legendary Opium War.

Over the next few years, British warships battered the Chinese imperial troops and local militias. One after another, China's port cities fell, unable to defend against their enemy's devastating cannon fire and superior naval technology. China, humiliated and demoralized, surrendered in 1842 and agreed to the terms set out in The Treaty of Nanking.

The treaty was a raw deal. China was forced to pay several million dollars worth of silver as reparations and to cede the city of Hong Kong, a strategic harbour to unload goods, to England.

This move also allowed the British to open up several Chinese trade ports (including Shanghai) and strip away China's economic protectionism, opening the country to foreign influence. Interestingly enough, opium was not mentioned in the treaty. Issues with the addictive substance, as well as the totally unfair treaty terms, led to the Second Opium War in 1856.

In the fallout from the Nanking treaty, the social and economic conditions in China deteriorated. Imperial administration became weak, public works (such as granaries to help people during drought years) were discontinued because of the costly war, and banditry and looting were rampant.

China's growing population exacerbated this chaotic situation. One estimate suggests that China's population nearly doubled between 1750 and 1850, from around 250 million to 410 million. Despite many more mouths to feed, farming production failed to grow enough. Toss in numerous floods, famines and natural disasters, and you've got a recipe for a collapsing country.

The southern province of Guangdong was one of the hardest hit areas. Despite being about the physical size of the state of Wyoming, it had a population of 16 million in 1787. By 1911, that number nearly doubled to about 31 million people. Only 10 percent of Guangdong's land was arable, driving up the market price of rice and making it difficult for poor families to afford to eat. Land distribution was shamefully unequal, with only a few wealthy owner families (who passed on property from generation to generation) and several million impoverished tenant farmers.

The opening of China to the West also destroyed Guangdong's cottage industries and domestic textile manufacturers, as cheap, high-volume, machine-made goods from Europe became favoured over local, hand-crafted products. Perhaps a little ironic, given today's context, no? It's little surprise then that the overwhelming majority of immigrants to Canada during this era were from Guangdong, specifically from Canton and its neighbouring counties.

Emigration from China was uncommon before the 19th century because the empire maintained strict controls. Citizens had been forbidden to leave the country since the Qing Dynasty in 1644. Surrounded by rebellious forces and hostile neighbours, China's government officials were paranoid that people would spill some dirt about China or somehow betray them if they emigrated. An official decree stated that anyone caught leaving China for foreign lands would be beheaded. Anyone in an authority position allowing people to leave would also be beheaded. I'm sure that if imperial soldiers had possessed the ability to telepathically read minds, people would have lost their heads for even thinking about leaving China.

China's anti-emigration policies continued until the mid-19th century. By that time, Western countries had developed a taste for cheap Chinese labour, and China, weakened by years of famine, warfare and rampant opium addiction, was nudged into signing agreements that gave Chinese people the right to leave the country.

Many citizens faced the harrowing choice of having to leave their homes, risk dying of starvation or meeting a bloody end. Unrest among the peasants had grown to a fever pitch, culminating with the Taiping Rebellion, and a frightening revolt led to civil war. In the end, after 14 years of violence, the Qing government needed help from the British and French to quell the insurrection. By this time, around 20 million people had lost their lives. Let me repeat: 20 million. It's hard to fathom.

These events and factors led to the first wave of mass migration out of China. Scholars would later refer to this event as the Great Chinese Diaspora. The majority of emigrants relocated to Southeast Asia or Latin America. But when news of North America's gold rushes reached China, the Chinese set sail for North America. It began as a trickle, not a flow. Three Chinese pioneers were reported to have arrived in California in 1848. One year later, there were 54, and, by the end of 1851, there were an estimated 4000 Chinese in the state, according to the Oakland Museum of California.

COMING TO CANADA

By the end of 1852, 25,000 Chinese were in California, almost all men, and most of them worked as gold miners and labourers. When gold was discovered along the Fraser River in 1858, the Chinese began making their way northward from California, and the term "Gold Mountain" stretched with them. Others even arrived by chartered ships from Hong Kong and Macao. They often landed first in Victoria, a launching pad that many of these gold diggers used to get to mainland British Columbia. (Formerly known as New Caledonia, the mainland became the Colony of British Columbia on August 2, 1858; a separate Colony of Vancouver Island existed from 1849 to 1866.) Estimates of BC's Chinese population in 1860 range from 1700 to 4000.

But some decided to remain in Victoria. These Chinese quickly established Canada's first Chinatown, on Cormorant Street (between Government and Douglas streets), the second oldest Chinatown in North America after San Francisco's. Initially, Victoria's Chinatown was mostly composed of spartan wooden huts and boarding houses where the miners stayed before going to the Fraser River area. Few of the early immigrants spoke any English, so interacting with Canadians socially was difficult. Most Chinese immigrants were so poor and uneducated they could barely read or write Chinese. But pretty soon, Chinese-run shops and services related to the mining industry and general frontier life began popping up. The little Chinese community provided some measure of comfort for these pioneers.

So what was working life like for a Chinese person in Canada during this time? Pretty darn tough. While some arrived as independent workers, many Chinese in North America at this point were temporary, contracted labourers, referred to pejoratively as "coolies."

Around this time, pre-Confederation Canada was rapidly expanding industrially. Commercial mining companies needed an affordable and plentiful workforce to do the dirty, dangerous jobs white workers didn't want to do.

The Chinese quickly became an attractive option. Chinese miners were given enough money for a boat ticket and a small stipend to keep them going until they landed in North America, usually at the ports of San Francisco or Victoria. Upon arrival, they were paid a wage, typically half of what a white worker received. Some Chinese didn't even get paid—the company was obligated to provide clothes and other bare necessities in return for a short-term contract. These indentured labourers worked for a term of five or ten years and were then released to work for themselves.

When the Chinese workers left the company, some went on to mine independently, usually picking over the sites abandoned by previous diggers, while others found employment as domestic help or took menial jobs. Very few Chinese worked as tradesmen, although some ended up as tailors and cobblers in BC's mining towns.

In these early days, the Chinese certainly faced discrimination but also had more than a few supporters among the general Canadian populace. Well, they received support as long as they did the dirty jobs and kept to themselves. The Chinese were seen as culturally and intellectually inferior, but they worked so hard that some Westerners publicly expressed admiration (albeit of the grudging variety) for their tireless work ethic and perseverance.

An article in the Victoria *British Colonist* in 1861 recognized that having the Chinese around was advantageous:

> We have plenty of room for many thousands of Chinamen. And notwithstanding they may not bring their wives with them to settle permanently in the country, nor build school-houses, churches, or acquire our language, but continue to live and work among themselves, yet there can be no shadow of a doubt but their industry enables them to add very largely to our own revenues....

One Western reporter for the *British Colonist* in 1866 wrote, "Chinese industry often triumphs where British indolence gives up. These men who produce the sample may be styled lucky where the truth is they worked at times when white men with just as fair chances were idling around..."

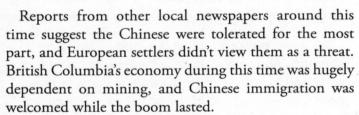

The Chinese began coming to Canada in significant numbers after gold was found along the Fraser River in BC in the late 1850s.

Reports from other local newspapers around this time suggest the Chinese were tolerated for the most part, and European settlers didn't view them as a threat. British Columbia's economy during this time was hugely dependent on mining, and Chinese immigration was welcomed while the boom lasted.

But, of course, the gold rush didn't last. By the mid-1860s, known deposits had been exhausted, and the province headed toward recession. Many European miners left Canada for the United States or returned home, and during this period, more workers were leaving Canada than were coming in. Canada's overall population was growing, but the portion of British Columbia's population centred on the mining industry suffered massive declines between the 1850s and 1870s. And because immigration from Europe to North America was costly, fresh European workers whose ships made landfall in the United States often never bothered going north.

With less work available, the Chinese were no longer seen as useful but instead were seen as competitors, especially because they were willing to accept far less money than white workers. The Chinese, because of their different skin colour, obvious cultural differences and resourcefulness, were easy to mark as scapegoats for the recession. Starting in the 1870s, newspaper coverage in Victoria about the Chinese noticeably changed in tone, according to sociologist Peter Li, author of *The Chinese in Canada*. The media now tended to focus on crimes committed by the Chinese, and editorials criticized their allegedly unrefined behaviour and inferior culture.

Despite the end of the gold rush and the mounting anti-Chinese resentment, many Chinese stayed in Canada, finding jobs as general labourers, coal miners or gardeners, or opening small laundry businesses or market stores. They defied the "sojourner" tag that the general Canadian public had attributed to the Chinese. Many Canadians had thought of the Chinese as temporary workers who had come just to strike it rich, or at least try to, and then return to their wives and families. They were believed to be in flux, with no intention of putting down roots in a country and culture so different from their native China. In part, this perception that the Chinese had no intention of settling down here may have initially made Canadians more welcoming to the Chinese.

And it's probably true that most Chinese did come to Canada with the intention of working hard, saving as much as they could and then returning to their homeland. But hardly any Chinese workers became rich, and few could afford to return home. Many were in this country to stay.

Gold Mountain was just the beginning of the Chinese influx into Canada. Over the next few years, several thousand more Chinese were brought in to tackle one of the most important nation-building projects in Canadian history. Whether Canadians at the time liked it or not, the monumental task of building a national railway would guarantee a significant ongoing Chinese presence in Canada.

CHAPTER THREE

THE CANADIAN PACIFIC RAILWAY AND THE HEAD TAX

I n the early 1870s, Canada was still a young country with plenty of promise. But its people and industries needed to be connected—both metaphorically and literally. John A. Macdonald, Canada's first prime minister, understood this, and his proposed solution aimed to address both issues.

A national system of railways, Macdonald argued, would link the burgeoning manufacturing industries in eastern Canada with the raw materials of western Canada. The railway would give Canada some measure of independence from the U.S., as the country's industries could avoid paying American tolls and freights. Macdonald also believed the railway would become a national symbol, something real and tangible that Canadians could be proud of.

When the Maritime provinces agreed to join the Dominion, Macdonald's government coordinated the construction of the Intercolonial Railway. It took just under a decade to complete. When it opened for business in 1876, the railway stretched from Truro, Nova Scotia, to Sainte-Flavie, Québec.

When Manitoba and British Columbia joined Confederation, they too were promised a railway that linked them to central and eastern Canada. Macdonald boldly announced a 10-year deadline to complete the Canadian Pacific Railway (CPR). He made this ambitious project a key tenet of his National Policy, a multi-step approach to nation building (the other steps included introducing tariffs to protect young domestic industries and encouraging immigration from Europe—not China, though).

The Intercolonial Railway in eastern Canada proved to be a cakewalk compared to the construction of the new railway in western Canada. Construction crews had to battle against the geography of Canada: the Laurentian Shield, with its vast forested lands and rivers north of Lake Superior, provided difficult engineering challenges, as did the Rocky Mountains and the canyons associated with the Thompson and Fraser rivers. The labour required for this undertaking was enormous, and the financial burden was a heavy one.

Work on the railway didn't actually begin for several years though. Macdonald became embroiled in a bribery scandal after it was alleged his Conservative government accepted political donations in return for the railway-building contract. The Liberals, who weren't crazy about the ultra-expensive railway in the first place, toppled the government, and Alexander Mackenzie became prime minister. Mackenzie's Liberals were obligated to continue the project, the land surveys having been done as early as 1871, but they were far less enthusiastic about it.

On the strength of his National Policy, Macdonald regained power in 1878, but the construction of his beloved railway had fallen way behind and was in serious jeopardy of fizzling out completely. The project finally began moving forward again. Canada had begun to pull out of a terrible economic depression, and the Canada-Pacific project regained political support. Railway contracts were handed out across the country.

In 1879, Andrew Onderdonk, an experienced engineer from New York, was awarded contracts to build most of the British Columbia portion of the railway, between Port Moody and Eagle Pass, a distance of more than 550 kilometres.

Laying rail in this region took a Herculean effort. The land was mountainous, and explosives were needed to clear the heavy rock. Onderdonk estimated he would need 10,000 men to get the job done, which at the time was nearly one-tenth of the province's entire population.

In the beginning, Onderdonk strictly recruited white men from California, but he found their performance lacking. Most of the workers were unemployed clerks or bartenders and were not used to the rigors of outdoor labour.

Onderdonk had previously supervised railway construction in the U.S. and had hired inexpensive, reliable Chinese labourers to complete sections of the railways for companies such as Central Pacific and Union Pacific. He remembered how efficient the Chinese workers were, so he brought in thousands of Chinese from Canada, the U.S. and overseas to help supply the workforce he desperately needed.

Between 1876 and 1880—immediately before construction of the transcontinental CPR began—only 2326 Chinese arrived in Canada by ship. But the numbers rose to nearly 3000 in 1881 and over 8000 in 1882, before tapering off to 2223 in 1884.

Of the 16,000 Chinese estimated to have entered Canada between 1881 and 1884, up to 6500 worked on the western sections of the CPR at any one time, alongside thousands of European and First Nations workers. By using Chinese workers, Onderdonk saved himself about $4 million. He would likely have gone bankrupt without them.

ANTI-CHINESE SENTIMENT

It wasn't easy for Onderdonk to acquire the Chinese labourers he needed to complete the railway. The anti-Chinese sentiment in British Columbia had been building for some time, and many white workers and their unions protested the hiring of more Chinese. Residents of British Columbia, who had somewhat welcomed the Chinese at the outset of the gold rush, began lobbying their government to keep them out during the punishing recession that followed. As early as 1860, the Colony of Vancouver Island tried introducing legislation forcing all new Chinese immigrants to pay $10—a head tax. It was defeated because many politicians recognized the courts would deem it unconstitutional.

In 1871, just before BC joined Confederation, the colonial legislature voted on a motion to force Chinese immigrants to pay a $50 fee. This, too, was defeated. The following year, a piece of legislation attempting to exclude Chinese labour on public works projects also failed to pass. In 1875, the BC legislature successfully passed one piece of anti-Chinese legislature—a new law that stripped Chinese Canadians of the right to vote in provincial elections.

Despite several ineffective attempts at taxing Chinese immigrants, BC politicians continued pressing hard on the issue. In 1878, the legislature proposed imposing a special tax of $10 on Chinese Canadians. It passed, but the courts later deemed it unconstitutional. There were other acts designed to regulate the presence and influence of Chinese in Canada: an act to prevent more Chinese immigration into BC as well as an act to prevent Chinese from acquiring Crown land. These racist policies never took hold, either.

Anti-Chinese attitudes were echoed in much of the newspaper coverage around this time. "Chinese competition unequal, immoral, and vicious!" screamed a *Mainland Guardian* headline in 1879. Finally, John A. Macdonald put his foot down on the matter. "At present it is simply a question of alternatives—either you must have this labour or you cannot have the railway," he said in the House of Commons in 1882.

Macdonald may have been viewed as a notorious drunkard, but he was among the most sober-minded on this issue. There was absolutely no way the western leg of the railway was going to get done without help from the Chinese. Just like during the gold rush, Canada lacked the necessary manpower and relied heavily on immigrants and First Nations workers to shore up the labour force.

The Chinese were popular hires for two main reasons. First, Chinese workers were affordable, working for about $1 per day and paying for their own food, camping and cooking gear out of pocket. They maintained their own tents and subsisted on a meagre diet of rice, dried salmon and tea. White Canadian workers were paid about twice as much and had many of their expenses covered.

Between 1881 and 1885, thousands of Chinese workers were hired to work on the Canadian Pacific Railway, like this section near Rogers Pass in BC.

The second reason for hiring the Chinese had to do with their outstanding work ethic. They diligently went about their tasks, rested as much as they could when the workday ended and then got up the next day to do it all over again. Some Westerners observed the marked differences in behaviour between the Chinese and white labourers during down time. While the white workers were keen to get their drink on, the Chinese kept quietly to themselves. According to a report in *The Port Moody Gazette* in 1885:

> A thousand white men lately employed on the railroad rushed out of the cars and into the saloons. In two hours the streets were full of lunatics; they roared and raved and attempted to force their way into private houses.

Twelve hundred Chinese arrived by the same train and went into the woods, and cooked their rice. It is amusing to see the difference between Pagans and Christians.

In addition to working hard and for very little pay, the Chinese men were usually given the most arduous, life-threatening jobs nobody else wanted to do. Building railways in BC at that time was dangerous work because workers had to blast through mountains in order to create tunnels, with only nodding attention to assuring their safety.

I recall watching those Canadian Heritage Minute clips on CBC television in the early 1990s. Each of the 60-second short films dramatized a defining moment in Canadian history, from James Naismith's invention of basketball to Jacques Plantes wearing the first goalie mask to Laura Secord risking her life to warn the British of an impending American attack during the war of 1812.

The one I remember most vividly is the clip about Chinese railway workers using nitroglycerine, in its liquid form, to clear rubble for tunnelling. Nitroglycerine was less expensive than dynamite but much less stable. Chinese workers were asked to carry small jars of the volatile substance into the dark tunnels and set the charges. But a slight bump could trigger a fierce explosion, and there were many deadly accidents. Landslides resulting from the blasts also buried people alive.

"They say there is one dead Chinese man for every mile of the track," an elderly Chinese grandfather tells his young grandkids in the Heritage clip.

It's not known exactly how many Chinese men died building the railway, however. In addition to the hazards of detonating explosives, many workers died from hypothermia, malnutrition and inadequate medical care.

Some Chinese workers were also killed in violent altercations with white workers, as the climate of racism was high during the time. One commonly cited estimate puts the death toll at around 1500, or about 10 percent of the Chinese workers brought in. Suffice to say, Canada would never have had its national railway were it not for Chinese blood on the tracks.

THE COMPLETION OF THE CPR

John A. Macdonald had promised that a national railway could be built in 10 years, but with the help of Chinese labour, the CPR was completed in an astonishing four years. The ceremonial "Last Spike" was driven into the ground on November 7, 1885, at Craigellachie in Eagle Pass, British Columbia. None of the Chinese who had been so instrumental in building the CPR were invited to attend the ceremony.

Where were they? Well, after completing the railway, many Chinese workers found themselves scattered across western Canada. Andrew Onderdonk had initially promised many Chinese labourers a one-way ticket back to China, but these tickets failed to materialize.

In November 1885, the Executive Council of British Columbia sent a report to the Secretary of State in Ottawa describing the hardship endured by many Chinese who were let go after finishing the railway:

> Thousands of these people, having been summarily discharged by the railway contractors, and their earnings having been absorbed by their rapacious masters or owners, are now left in a starving condition, and unless substantial relief be extended to them there is every prospect of their perishing during the winter.

(Public Archives of Canada, 1886)

The Chinese working camps that lined the railway disbanded, and the many unemployed Chinese, enduring malnutrition and fatigue, were stranded and forced to fend for themselves. Many took up casual employment in British Columbia's logging, mining, farming and canning industries. But a brutal recession would engulf British Columbia for the next two decades, making jobs hard to find. The situation got so bad during the late 19th century that the Chinese Consolidated Benevolent Association in Victoria actually made attempts to discourage immigration from China.

Workers who had enough money saved up mostly chose to sail back to China, but the less fortunate either crowded into British Columbia's few Chinatowns or journeyed onward to other parts of Canada. The first Chinese pioneers arrived in Alberta in 1885, establishing small Chinese communities in cities across the province. The Chinese slowly filtered across the rest of Canada in the ensuing years.

The CPR that the Chinese and others had worked so tirelessly to build did much for our burgeoning nation. As John A. Macdonald had predicted, it linked together Canada's resources, industries and people and became a national symbol. The building of the railway is immortalized in songs, poems and films. For the 1967 Centennial, Gordon Lightfoot, one of Canada's legendary singer-songwriters, penned a famous tune called the "Canadian Railroad Trilogy." His verses paid tribute to the many men who worked on those rails.

It took several decades before the Chinese in particular received the public recognition they deserved. In September 1989, the CPR corporation erected a monument in downtown Toronto dedicated to the Chinese labourers. Built near the Rogers' Centre (then called the

Sky Dome), the monument features metal statues of Chinese workers pushing and pulling giant wooden pillars. It's not unusual to see wreaths lying at the foot of the memorial, as Chinese associations continue to pay their respects today. A portion of the monument's poignant inscription reads:

> Dedicated to the Chinese railroad workers who helped construct the Canadian Pacific Railway through the Rocky Mountains of Alberta and British Columbia thus uniting Canada geographically and politically....Far from their families, amid hostile sentiments, these men laboured long hours and made the completion of the railway physically and economically possible....With no means of going back to China when their labour was no longer needed, thousands drifted in near destitution along the completed track. All of them remained nameless in the history of Canada. We erect this monument to remember them.

On May 27, 2005, the CPR recognized the Chinese again by naming a rail interchange in Kamloops, British Columbia, after a Chinese labourer named Cheng Ging Butt.

Cheng was born in Guangdong and came to Canada at the age of 23. He began working on the railway in 1881 and saw the project through to its completion. After the railway was finished, Cheng settled in Yale, British Columbia, where he set up a dry goods store and farmed cherries, often selling his products to railway staff. He got married and raised eight sons and two daughters before passing away in 1930 at the age of 72.

Cheng's biography may not seem that remarkable, but given the historical context of the time, his life was a small miracle. He arrived in Canada as a young man, survived the gruelling work on the rails and then managed to carve out a living in this country during a time when the Chinese were subject to open discrimination. Perhaps the most inspiring part of his story was that at the grand unveiling of the new Cheng Interchange, several of Cheng's descendents—now third- and fourth-generation Canadians—were on hand to watch.

As the monument in Toronto observed, most of the thousands of Chinese railway workers who helped to unite our country will tragically go nameless in the history of Canada. I'm sure many of their ghosts still walk the rails. But at least someone recognized that Cheng Ging Butt had a name, and I'm sure some of those long-forgotten Chinese pioneers would have taken a little comfort in that.

THE HEAD TAX

As the railway was nearing completion, Canadian politicians became increasingly anxious about the "Chinese question." As there would no longer be a need for Chinese labour, the call for cutting Chinese immigration became louder than ever. The federal government launched a Royal Commission in 1884 to assess what was to be done with the thousands of Chinese now living in Canada.

The popular argument against the Chinese was that they were too foreign, too different, and would be unable to assimilate into Canada. "The main objection to the Chinese is that they are not of our race and cannot become a part of ourselves," said Hugh Nelson, a senator from British Columbia. "We cannot build up a homogenous people in Canada with races of that description, a population totally alien to ours."

The tide of public resentment against the Chinese was rising fast, although some people of good conscience decried such bigotry and fear mongering. The Honourable Mr. Justice Henry P. Pellew Crease, Judge of the Supreme Court of British Columbia, observed that the anti-Chinese fervour being drummed up was not rational behaviour but a political tactic (and using fear to attract votes is a strategy that unfortunately continues to work well even today). Crease stated before the Royal Commission in 1884:

> The outcry against the Chinese takes its rise in a great measure in the efforts of persons, who for political motives, are desirous of posing themselves as the friends of the working classes, through their sweet votes to gain political power and influence. All political parties, the "ins" as well as the "outs," aim at this; and through the press and orations, and even no little misrepresentation, exaggerate.

Initially, politicians in other parts of the country largely resisted supporting anti-Chinese policies because they didn't experience the influx of Chinese that British Columbia had. After all, about 98 percent of all Chinese in Canada were in British Columbia during the gold rush and railway era. But in 1885, after years of pressure from politicians out west, the federal government finally imposed a head tax of $50 on Chinese immigrants. It was the first federal anti-Chinese bill ever to be passed, effectively discouraging new Chinese from entering. The tax also applied to Chinese who were already living in Canada.

The justification behind pushing such a discriminatory measure on a group of people was simple in the minds of the politicians. The Chinese were just workhorses, living machines, and consequently were not owed the rights or liberties due to other residents of Canada. Prime Minister John A. Macdonald told the House of Commons that the Chinese worker, "has no common interest with us, and while he gives us labour he is paid for it, and is valuable, the same as a threshing machine or any other agricultural implement which we may borrow from the United States on hire and return it to the owner on the south side of the line...he has no British instincts or British feelings or aspirations, and therefore ought not to have a vote."

How much would $50 have been worth in 1885? Although online calculators offer limited financial data pertaining to the years before 1914, ballpark estimates suggest it would have been the equivalent of a little over $1000 today, which is a bit surprising. Although this amount may not seem like a staggering amount today, it probably was to many of the Chinese Canadians stuck in menial jobs and overseas Chinese wishing to make the journey to this country. This tax doesn't seem entirely insurmountable. But the first head tax wasn't necessarily designed to kick out all the Chinese.

By the late 1800s, the economy had picked up, and both white and Chinese labour were available in abundance. But given the relative economic and labour instabilities during this period, government officials and industry leaders felt it would be prudent to maintain a large base of convenient, cheap Chinese labour. They also wanted to limit the number of new Chinese immigrants, who were seen as culturally incompatible with Canadian society.

A simple way to achieve this end was to stem the flow of immigration and to deny the Chinese already here any substantial rights as Canadians. As sociologist Peter Li concluded, the head tax "was a means of ensuring that the supply of Chinese labour would not be completely severed, while at the same time officially endorsing the second-class entrance status of the Chinese. This endorsement helped to sustain the marginal participation of the Chinese in the Canadian economy."

It was a sneaky tactic. The head tax wasn't large enough to cause most Chinese to flee the country, but it was substantial enough to permanently mark them as second-class citizens. Because they weren't "real Canadians" (white), it was believed the Chinese would be less inclined to demand things other Canadians were granted: equal wages with white workers, access to education and medical attention and the chance to advance their station in life. The general public already saw the Chinese as incapable of integrating into Canadian society, and the head tax was the government's political legitimization of that perception.

In addition to the various institutional and social controls the government gained by introducing the head tax, this discriminatory policy also lined the federal coffers quite handsomely. A few Chinese were exempt—some wealthy merchants, visiting students and clergymen were allowed in free because they either brought money with them or were here temporarily. During World War I, the Canadian government also exempted workers from mainland China who were taken through Canada to assist the Commonwealth in labour operations in Europe and Africa. Between 1886 and 1894, over 12,000 Chinese paid taxes and registration fees, generating $624,679 of revenue for the government.

Federal officials, however, likely underestimated exactly how badly the Chinese wanted to come to Canada. Over the next 10 years, more than 30,000 Chinese entered the country and paid the fee, leading to about $2.4 million in tax revenue.

The $50 tax had failed to discourage immigration, so in the Chinese Immigration Act of 1900, the fee was doubled to $100. Three years later, the tax increased five-fold to $500—equivalent to two years of wages for a typical Chinese worker. With such a heavy price to pay, the inflow of Chinese immigrants slowed down after 1903. But still, nearly 40,000 Chinese paid the head tax between 1904 and 1924.

The head tax was eventually shelved, but only because it was replaced by an even more discriminatory measure—the Chinese Immigration Act of 1923, which stopped Chinese immigration almost entirely. By the time this happened, the Canadian government had collected around $23 million from about 82,000 Chinese people in Canada.

It's amazing that so many Chinese chose to pay the tax despite its size and unfairness. They paid to live in a country that only tolerated them because they'd do the physically taxing, menial jobs nobody else wanted. How many families were kept separated by this entrance fee? How many lonely Chinese people worked themselves to the bone in hopes of being able to send a boat ticket over so they could reunite with their loved ones? By 1931, there were 1240 men to every 100 women in Chinese Canadian communities. Census data shows that, sadly, most of the men were married, but their wives were left behind in China.

All of Canada's ethnic minorities have had to contend with prejudice and inequality during their early years in this country, including white European settlers. Unfortunately, xenophobia and turning immigrants into scapegoats appear to be recurring themes in the early history of our country. But the head tax against the Chinese remains one of the most shameful examples of discrimination by our government.

Chinese organizations, including the Chinese Canadian National Council, and Chinese Canadian politicians began lobbying Ottawa in the early 1980s to offer redress to those people directly affected by the head tax. The national campaigns included attendance at community meetings, presentations at schools and attracting attention to the issue through the media.

But perhaps the most memorable campaign came when Gim Wong, an 82-year-old Vancouver man, embarked on a cross-country motorcycle "ride for redress." Wong, a World War II veteran, rode his Harley-Davidson from Victoria to Ottawa in 2005 as a tribute to his father, who had paid the head tax many years earlier. Because Wong's father had to pay the massive fee, it took him 13 years to be able to afford to bring his wife over from China. At the end of his month-long ride, he delivered a petition to Parliament asking the government to pay $21,000 to any living head taxpayers.

It wasn't until the following year, under Prime Minister Stephen Harper, that the federal government finally recognized the injustice of its policy. On June 22, 2006, Harper rose in the House of Commons and offered a full apology to Chinese Canadians who were forced to pay the head tax. He also announced that the government would be making symbolic individual payments of $20,000 to the surviving Chinese who paid the fee, or to their surviving spouses, and that several million dollars would be put toward launching historical recognition programs as a tribute to those Chinese.

During his short speech, Harper said Canadians had "the collective responsibility to build a country based firmly on the notion of equality of opportunity, regardless of one's race or ethnic origin."

We, along with most Canadians, have recognized that this past measure constituted a moral blemish on Canada's soul. After all the Chinese Canadian community has contributed to this country over the years—from the great national railway forward—you were deserving of nothing less. It's no exaggeration to say that the Canada we know and love today would not exist without your efforts.

His sentiments, obviously a far cry from his Conservative Party predecessor John A. Macdonald, were appreciated by members of the country's Chinese Canadian communities. Whether or not this gesture is enough is another question.

CHAPTER FOUR

LIFE IN CANADA, THE GREAT WAR AND THE EXCLUSION ACT

As the Chinese spread across Canada, incoming immigrants met up with their friends and families, establishing small Chinese communities. By 1891, about 9000 Chinese lived in British Columbia, 31 in Manitoba, 97 in Ontario and 36 in Québec. By 1901, more than 17,000 Chinese lived in Canada.

But no matter where they settled, the jobs they found were as unglamorous as you can imagine: ditch-digging, peddling fruits and vegetables, shoemaking and house-keeping. According to census data in 1921, nearly 48 percent of Chinese Canadians were menial labourers or servants, while a mere five percent were in the professional or merchant classes. Two of the most common ways for a Chinese person to earn a living were to work in a salmon cannery or to start a laundry.

During the early 20th century, salmon exports became one of British Columbia's most valuable trade commodities, along with lumber and precious metals. The province's first canneries started up in the 1870s alongside the Fraser River, in Delta, near Vancouver. By 1889, nearly 60 canneries were in operation, from Vancouver Island to the Alaska border. Thanks to innovations in canning technology and the growing demand for canned food in industrial Europe, salmon canning became one of the fastest growing and most lucrative industries.

But what made it possible for the salmon canning industry boom, as with mining and railway construction, was the cheap and readily available Chinese labour. The early canneries were expensive to operate and were susceptible to other factors, such as how plentiful the salmon catch was that year. Few white Canadians wanted to work in such a tiring, unstable and seasonal job—most canning happened in summer—so the Chinese stepped in.

Canning was a difficult, laborious and no doubt smelly task, especially before machines came into wide use. The cans had to be cut from sheet tinplate, then formed and soldered—all by hand. In the late 19th century, a typical cannery, employing 100 to 150 men, could manufacture 700,000 cans in two months. Butchering the fish and filling the cans were also done by hand, as were building the wooden shipping crates that held the cans.

As more canneries began opening up around the world, prices fluctuated, further making canning an even less appealing career choice. That Chinese workers were willing to accept lower wages helped lend stability to this emerging Canadian industry. The Chinese came to dominate canning work, accounting for about three-quarters of the industry's labour force by 1900. Actually, the Chinese became so synonymous with canning that, when a revolutionary mechanized processing device was introduced in the early 1900s, it was dubbed "The Iron Chink." It was a terribly derogatory name for an otherwise nifty machine that looked like a giant wheel with blades and that could behead and clean salmon 10 times as fast as a Chinese worker.

Another common job for a Chinese person at this time was washing clothes. The first Chinese laundries emerged during the gold rush to service the miners in the

Sam Wing stands outside a Chinese laundry in Innisfail, Alberta, in 1904. By 1921, there were nearly 6000 Chinese laundries operating across Canada.

towns of Barkerville and Yale. Vancouver had a Chinese laundry, the Wah Chong laundry, before the city was incorporated in 1886. These Chinese-run "wash houses" soon spread across Canada, especially to rural areas where steam laundries weren't yet available. By 1921, nearly 6000 Chinese laundries were operating across Canada, according census data from that period. Over 2000 of them were being run in Ontario, while the prairie provinces had around 500 each.

Washing clothes for a living, by hand, was hard work. In his 1926 book *Oriental Immigration to Canada*, Cheng Tien-Fang, a visiting scholar from China, interviewed the workers at many of these laundries. The laundry workers, he found, usually worked 11- or 12-hour days, keeping their stores open as long as customers would come in. They charged 20 to 30 percent less per shirt than the larger white establishments. Offering lower prices didn't make any of them wealthy, though; because Chinese laundry workers hand-washed everything, they could clean only so much clothing in a day. The maximum a laundryman could make each month was around $150, equivalent to about $1800 today.

In *Enduring Hardship: The Chinese Laundry in Canada*, author Ban Seng Hoe recounted a conversation with a Winnipeg man named Ho King, who came to Canada in 1918 and immediately began working at his father's laundry. By 1926, he took over the family business and worked there until he retired in the 1970s.

Ho King recalled the exhausting, "painful" work involved in running a laundry. Workers would rise at 6:00 AM to light a fire in the stove and boil water. "We had to boil the water in a big pot and then poured it into the washing machine. It was a very hard work." After washing the clothes, King would hang them up to dry. Then he'd iron the clothes, a difficult process involving heavy irons he had to heat manually over a potbelly stove. In addition to his washing duties, King had to chop wood for the stoves, take deliveries of coal and keep the fires going. Because of the low income and long hours, his laundry was not only his business but was also his home—his entire life.

Like the miners and railway workers who came before them, Chinese laundrymen faced intense hostility from white workers who felt the Chinese were invading their turf. In 1902, the Laundry Workers' Union of Nelson, BC, appealed to the Royal Commission on Chinese and Japanese Immigration to do something about the "direct Mongolian competition":

> In the laundry work in Nelson alone there were at the lowest estimate two hundred Chinamen employed at a wage varying from 75 cents to $1.50 per day, their hours of labour extending over the whole twenty-four hours, with barely time to eat and sleep. In some wash-houses, a double gang is worked, the off men sleeping in the same apartment as those working, and often sleeping on clothes to be washed; and their habits are such that we feel sure that in many cases a health officer would condemn the same as injurious to public health....We extend our most hearty approval and support to any legislation which will effectually remove this evil of Mongolian labour.

Racial tension was high, especially on the West Coast, where most Chinese people in Canada lived. One of the ugliest incidents happened in 1907 in Vancouver, when an anti-Asian organization incited deadly riots in the city's Chinese and Japanese ethnic enclaves. The Asiatic Exclusion League (AEL) had originated in San Francisco, where many Chinese in the U.S. first settled. It soon spread to British Columbia and was composed mostly of local trade and labour groups.

In addition to the build-up of resentment for Chinese immigrants in British Columbia, a recent influx of Japanese workers into the area sent racial antipathy through the roof. The Japanese, like the Chinese, were viewed as unassimilable and undesirable. But with Japan's victory over Russia in the Russo–Japanese War in 1905, the Japanese were soon regarded with a further dimension of suspicion and hostility.

On September 7, 1907, the AEL held a demonstration at Vancouver's City Hall. After working the crowd up into an anti-Asian frenzy, thousands of people made their way to the city's Chinatown. Forty years later, an article in *Vancouver Sun Magazine* re-created the scary scenario, as a monster parade marched down Hastings Street:

> First came the speakers and their lady sympathizers in horse-drawn carriages, followed by over 5000 marching men, each with a white badge fluttering from his button-hole….Then someone shouted "On to Chinatown!" and the trouble started….On the first trip only rocks were thrown and hundreds of windows were broken. The second trip proved more vicious, for this time there was gunfire. When the mob grew tired of this they moved down to Japtown. Here they met fierce resistance but there was no shooting….No Chinese or Japanese appeared on the streets for days.

The police cordoned off the "Oriental" sections of Vancouver and declared martial law. The day after the riot, hundreds of Chinese and Japanese armed themselves, buying up rifles, revolvers and knives. Thankfully, no more major violence occurred. It's hard to determine how many casualties there were: English newspapers suggested there were no fatalities and largely tried to downplay the severity of the riot, but the *Taiwan Daily News* later reported that Japanese merchants had killed four white men.

Later in 1907, the federal government held an inquiry into the Vancouver incident with a view to compensating the Asian shops and organizations affected by the mob swarming. William Lyon Mackenzie King, deputy minister of labour during this time, presided over the inquiry. In his final report, Mackenzie King agreed to award $9000 to Japanese businesses and $26,000 to Chinese merchants, whose stores had been more badly damaged.

In the end, the physical damage was significant—many shops had their windows smashed in and signs destroyed—but things could have been uglier. The real, lasting damage was to race relations in British Columbia. The Vancouver race riot is still commemorated by Asian groups more than 100 years after it occurred.

THE GREAT WAR

It was perfectly clear that the Canadian government was unwelcoming to the Chinese in the early 20th century, but naturalized Chinese Canadians and their Canadian-born children were loyal to their new country and were eager to prove it. When World War I broke out in 1914, many Chinese offered their services to the military. British Columbia, however, refused to take Chinese recruits, so a handful of Chinese travelled to Alberta and Ontario, the two provinces willing to accept them. Even by 1917, after Prime Minister Robert Borden retreated from his earlier promise and announced that conscription would be required, "Orientals" were still largely excluded from the draft.

Still, some courageous Chinese men in Canada found a way to enter the trenches. It's not known exactly how many of them served Canada in World War I, although one estimate pegs the number at around 300. Some people believe this number is a little inflated. At any rate, Chinese Canadians represented only a tiny fraction of Canada's total overseas military contingent of more than 600,000 men.

A few amazing stories about Chinese Canadians did emerge from the Great War. Several Chinese Canadian soldiers who survived were honoured for their heroic contributions. In her book *The Dragon and the Maple Leaf*, in which she profiled a few of them, Marjorie Wong included the extraordinary story of two brothers from Shuswap, British Columbia.

The Louie brothers, Wee Tan and Wee Hong, were born in Canada in the late 19th century. Despite the racial tension between the Chinese and white Canadians, both brothers wanted to serve their country and made more than a few sacrifices to do so. Because British Columbia wouldn't accept Wee Tan into the military, he went to Calgary to enlist. It took him three months to get there on horseback—a horse that he bought with savings he specifically set aside for this personal mission.

On his way to Calgary, Wee Tan chose an English name from a mail box he had passed by. Now calling himself William Thomas Louie, he enlisted with the 10th Canadian Infantry Battalion raised by the Calgary Regiment. He was soon shipped off to England for training. Because of his small stature and speed, William was put to work as a trench runner in France, The Netherlands and Belgium. It was an extremely danger-ous task, and he sustained serious, permanent injuries, including hearing loss from exploding artillery shells.

William survived the war and returned to Canada in March 1919. He was later honourably discharged and given the British War Medal and the Victory Medal.

William's brother, Hong Louie, served in France between 1917 and 1919, working first as a gunner and later as a wireless radio operator and driver. For his efforts, Hong was also presented with the British War Medal and the Victory Medal. After the war, he studied electrical engineering in Chicago and decided to settle in Orillia, Ontario, with the ambition of setting up his own electronics store.

Hong Louie applied for a shop licence but was refused because he was Chinese. He took the issue to the prime minister's office but didn't get anywhere. After this disappointment, he sent his war medals to then–Prime Minister Mackenzie King, along with a note stating that the discrimination he faced was not what he had gone to war for. Amazingly, King returned Hong's medals with a letter of apology, and Hong Louie received his licence. He ran the shop until he retired in 1976.

It's also possible that a platoon composed almost entirely of Chinese Canadians in the 52nd Battalion fought at the famous Third Battle at Ypres in 1917. Over 15,000 Canadians were killed over several months of bloody, muddy violence. This horrific battle, also known as the Battle of Passchendaele, would later inspire an award-winning film directed by and starring Calgary-born actor Paul Gross. Major General George Pearkes, a highly decorated veteran of the war, mentioned this Chinese Canadian platoon to history book author James Morton. But some people believe it's likely that Pearkes mistook Japanese volunteers in the 52nd Battalion for Chinese. Research indicates that several Japanese Canadians served with the battalion, but it remains unclear if anyone of Chinese origin did.

Chinese nationals also made an important contribution to the Commonwealth forces. Even before China formally declared war on Germany and Austria in 1917, Britain and France had recruited several thousand Chinese labourers to help them with a variety of hazardous but crucial operations in Europe, Africa and Mesopotamia (now Iraq). The men, mostly from China's northeastern Shandong province, were contracted to build dugouts, repair transport routes, dig trenches and provide general support for the frontline troops.

Some of the labour groups were shipped from China through the Panama and Suez canals and around South Africa, but going through Canada proved to be the easiest and safest route. Because most of the journey took place on land (by way of the CPR), the labourers were able to avoid ocean travel, and hence exposure to deadly German U-Boats. Over 84,000 Chinese men were brought secretly through Canada in sealed railway cars from Victoria, British Columbia, to Halifax, Nova Scotia. From Halifax, the workers boarded ships and headed to Europe. The Canadian government waived the $500 head tax for these workers, provided they were supervised by armed guards the entire time they were in the country.

There aren't many surviving accounts of those trips. According to Brad Cran, a Vancouver-based essayist and magazine editor, the Chinese labourers were treated relatively well. They were given bread when the rice supplies were depleted, and, after arriving at their destination, they reportedly shook hands in a jovial manner with the Canadian soldiers who had guarded them during the rail journey. One ugly incident did occur in 1919 at

William Head, a quarantine station near Victoria on Vancouver Island. A riot broke out when some Chinese workers got fed up after waiting several months to travel home. An unknown number escaped the holding pens and, presumably, began new lives in Canada.

PROHIBITED CLASSES

After World War I, Canada, like many other countries around the world, plunged into a deep recession. This particular economic slump was mercifully brief, as the Roaring Twenties—with its mass production, jazz music, art deco, bathtub gin and funny gangster accents—was just around the corner. But the recession lasted long enough to fan the flames of racial hostility, especially toward Asians.

With the war over, soldiers returned home in search of jobs and, just as with the gold rush and after the completion of the CPR, labour leaders and politicians heard complaints that cheap Chinese labour was preventing many white people from finding gainful employment. Another public concern was the growing number of Chinese owning land and farms. Astonishingly, the head tax, in effect since 1885, hadn't significantly curbed immigration from China. The Chinese population in Canada more than doubled between 1901 and 1921, growing from about 17,000 to nearly 37,000. By 1917–18, the tail end of the war, about 4000 Chinese were making their way to Canada annually.

By the early 1920s, the calls for Ottawa to completely shut down Chinese immigration were as loud as ever. And with a federal election looming in 1921, Canadian politicians responded in spades.

Having grown up in this country during the latter part of the 20th century, I was absolutely shocked to see the frightening level of racism featured in some of the election campaign advertising of the 1920s. In 1921, British Columbia's Liberal Party candidates took out a full-page ad in the *Vancouver Sunday Sun* announcing in bold-type font that "Liberal Candidates are pledged to a White British Columbia…they will make British Columbia a White Man's country." The ad speaks of "the domination of the Yellow Race" and how every job in British Columbia should be "occupied by the White man." This discriminatory message didn't come from an isolated chapter of a white supremacist group: it came from the Liberal Party. The same Liberal Party that is, according to its official mandate, "committed to the view that the dignity of each individual man and woman is the cardinal principle of democratic society…"

The Liberals went on to win that election, and William Lyon Mackenzie King (the same guy who, as deputy minister of labour, awarded the Chinese and Japanese merchants financial compensation for the Vancouver race riots) became prime minister. In 1923, Mackenzie King's government finally bowed to the intense pressure and passed the Chinese Immigration Act, also known as the Exclusion Act. According to the new measure, "No person of Chinese origin or descent unless he is a Canadian citizen…shall be permitted to enter or land in Canada, or having entered or landed in Canada shall be permitted to remain therein…"

The Chinese effectively became part of the "Prohibited Classes" and were grouped in with an assorted set of undesirables, including "idiots, epileptics, diseased persons, procurers, alcohol or drug addicts, illiterates, the mentally or physically defective, criminals, and persons of constitutional psychopathic inferiority." Idiots? Psychopathic inferiority? Many miraculous concepts were invented during the Roaring Twenties, but it appears that political correctness was not one of them.

The few exceptions to this outright ban were visiting students, diplomats and some wealthy merchants. In addition, fully documented Chinese Canadians had to give written notices to federal officials in order to visit China. If they were away from Canada for more than two years, they'd lose their citizenship. The Exclusion Act not only barred Chinese from coming to Canada but it also separated families who had been planning to build new lives here. As the Chinese population in Canada was predominately male at this time, many husbands who had been saving up to bring their wives over were now completely powerless to do so. During the 1920s and 1930s, Chinese males outnumbered Chinese females by more than 12 to one.

Of course, Chinese communities across Canada protested and rallied against the legislation, but it was passed with a startling political efficiency with which today's Canadians are entirely unfamiliar. The Act was introduced into the House of Commons in March 1923, assented to in late June and came into effect July 1—Dominion Day. After the Chinese Immigration Act was enacted, July 1 ceased to be a cause for celebration for Chinese Canadians. Dominion Day became "Humiliation Day," and for years afterward, many Chinese Canadians closed their businesses on this day to mark their dismay.

CHAPTER FIVE

WORLD WAR II: THE END OF EXCLUSION

C anada, as a country, experienced turbulent times throughout the 1920s and 1930s. The Roaring Twenties, an energetic decade of technological innovation, peace and prosperity, came spectacularly undone after the Wall Street Stock Market Crash of 1929. The sharp economic decline, combined with horrendous droughts in North America, led to the Great Depression, a period of time when Canada's gross national product fell an incredible 40 percent, and unemployment shot up to nearly 30 percent.

The rampant joblessness caused Chinese Canadians to struggle more than ever, as even the most menial jobs to which they were restricted dried up almost as quickly as the wheat crops in the Prairies. Welfare was extremely limited to the Chinese; in Alberta, for example, a Chinese Canadian typically received half the relief payment a white Canadian was given. In British Columbia, well over 100 Chinese Canadians died from starvation during the Great Depression.

For over two decades, since the Exclusion Act had passed in 1923, immigration from China to Canada ground to a halt, and the Chinese population in Canada began to decline, dropping from around 47,000 in 1931 to 35,000 in 1941. The severe economic conditions in Canada compelled thousands of Chinese to return to China and Hong Kong, where their wives and families were waiting. But many Chinese travelled back because they were concerned about the growing prospect of war between the Republic of China and the Empire of Japan.

China had been engulfed in a terrible conflict with Japan for several decades. Since the end of the First Sino-Japanese War in 1895, the two countries had engaged in battle intermittently during the 1930s, and Japan actually occupied several regions of China during this time. But full-scale warfare erupted in 1937 after an incident at the Marco Polo Bridge near China's capital, Beijing, when Japanese forces training near the bridge accused the Chinese of abducting one of their soldiers. The soldier was later found unharmed, but not before the tension between the opposing forces escalated and led to violence. Historians have debated at length whether this incident was unintentional or completely fabricated by the Japanese forces as an excuse to fight (and, apparently, going to war under false pretences is still in fashion).

Whatever the true cause, this misunderstanding directly led to the Second Sino-Japanese War that saw Japan invade China and infamously rape and massacre hundreds of thousands of civilians in the major city of Nanjing. The next year, the city of Canton in Guangdong (from where the majority of early Chinese immigrants to

Canada originated) also fell. By 1941, Japan controlled most of China's coastal regions.

During this time, conflicts also broke out in Europe. After Nazi Germany invaded Poland on September 1, 1939, Britain, France and the other Commonwealth countries quickly declared war. Canada, led by the re-elected William Lyon Mackenzie King, followed suit on September 10.

But it was on December 7, 1941, "a date that will live in infamy," that both the Asian and European wars merged into World War II. On that day, Japanese fighter pilots and navy ships attacked the American naval base at Pearl Harbor in the Hawaiian Islands. The swift, devastating strike caught the United States unawares. As Japan expanded its military control in the East, it was believed the United States would retaliate once Japan made moves to take British colonies in Southeast Asia. The Japanese military were certain a sudden, pre-emptive assault at this strategic base would keep the American navy from exerting their influence in the Pacific.

Less than eight hours after the Pearl Harbor assault, the Japanese attacked Hong Kong, a British colony since the end of the First Opium War. Hong Kong, a major trading port, had been effectively surrounded by Japanese forces since the fall of Canton in 1938. Britain had long been wary of Japan's growing aggression in the Far East and had been bolstering its garrison in Hong Kong before the attack. Hong Kong's defence troops included two Canadian battalions, the Royal Rifles of Canada from Québec City and the Winnipeg Grenadiers.

The Hong Kong Garrison defended the island fiercely, but they were outnumbered by Japanese imperial soldiers. In one famous act of Canadian bravery, Company Sergeant Major John Robert Osborne of the

Grenadiers threw himself onto an enemy grenade, saving the lives of the men around him. He was posthumously awarded with the Victoria Cross (the highest military honour a Commonwealth soldier can receive) and honoured with a statue in Hong Kong Park. For a while, however, it looked as though Osborne's sacrifice would be in vain. After days and days of punishing aerial bombardments and deadly fighting on the ground, the colony's governor, Sir Mark Aitchison Young, surrendered to the Japanese in person on December 25. The locals called it "Black Christmas."

It's likely that some of the 12,000 Chinese who returned to China between 1931 and 1941 did so in part to take up arms against a potential Japanese invasion. But Japan's dual attack on the United States and Hong Kong officially brought the Allies to war in Asia, and suddenly, both Canadians and Chinese had a common enemy.

How many Chinese Canadians signed on to fight in World War II is not clear. The most commonly reported numbers indicate that it was somewhere between 400 and 800. As during World War I, the contingent of Chinese Canadian soldiers was a tiny fraction of the 1.1 million Canadians who served overall. Still, Chinese Canadians fought bravely in Europe and played unique and important roles in some operations in the Pacific. Whether or not the Chinese Canadian contribution to the war was particularly significant, the events during and after World War II further strengthened the link between the Chinese and Canada.

For this war, most Chinese Canadians were able to voluntarily enlist for the army in their own provinces, although, at first, the Canadian government resisted sending the Chinese from British Columbia overseas. British Columbia still boasted the largest number of Chinese in the country, and many white Canadian residents and politicians were concerned that letting Chinese Canadians fight in the war would later give them the right to vote.

Chinese Canadians were also barred from serving in the air force until 1942 or from joining the navy until 1943. Up until those years, both military wings insisted that troops be of European descent.

It wasn't until 1944 that most Chinese Canadians were called into duty. Part of the Canadian military's change of heart was likely due to embarrassment. The federal government eventually acknowledged that several especially gung-ho Chinese Canadian soldiers had gone to the United States to see if they could sign on after being rejected at home. Another likely reason was that the British government was exerting a little pressure on the Canadian military because it had been interested in recruiting Chinese Canadians to work in their Special Operations Executive unit. This espionage team carried out missions in Southeast Asia, where pockets of ethnic Chinese resided. The Allies deemed it useful to have some Chinese-speaking soldiers at their disposal. For once, Chinese Canadians found that their ethnic heritage was an asset and not a liability.

The hundreds of Chinese Canadians who volunteered to serve the Special Operations Executive did so for a variety of reasons. One obvious motive was to gain some measure of revenge against the Japanese for invading China. Another reason (a stronger one, in my opinion) was to prove how committed the Chinese were to Canada, despite all the social, economic and political barriers that had been purposely placed in front of them. Canadian politician and historian Roy MacLaren described this remarkable patriotism in his book *Canadians Behind Enemy Lines 1939–1945:*

In volunteering for clandestine warfare, the spirit of adventure was as evident in them as it had been in those Canadians who went into occupied Europe. But for the young Chinese Canadians, their service meant something more. For them, it was also an affirmation of equality. Their parents, or even grandparents, as well as themselves, had been second-class Canadians, deprived of the full privileges of citizenship. They were ready, even eager, to fill all the obligations of citizenship so that in return they might receive all those rights under which other Canadians took for granted.

Indeed, many Chinese Canadians enlisted with the clear aim of gaining the vote, something denied to them for as long as they'd been in Canada. This issue became extremely contentious within the Chinese community, as many argued that they should not fight unless they already had the rights of every other Canadian citizen. A vigorous public debate in Vancouver took place to address the matter, with young Chinese Canadians eager to join the cause passionately justifying their decisions to the other members of their community who were sceptical that things could ever change for the Chinese.

Many years later in the documentary *Unwanted Soldiers* (1999), John Ko Bong, a Canadian war veteran born in Victoria, recalled attending that meeting. He said the hall was packed with about 200 people:

> We had to stand up and face the room full of young people and their parents questioning us: "What are the benefits?" "What are we going to get out of this?" "Who is going to guarantee us we are going to be treated as Canadians?" But I said this is the key that will open the door for us, because we'd be standing with our Canadian boys that we went to school with, shoulder-to-shoulder.

Alex Louie, another Chinese Canadian veteran featured in the documentary, shared John Ko Bong's belief. "We wanted to improve our lot, and in order to improve our lot, we had to do something extraordinary," Louie said.

And both Alex Louie and John Ko Bong would find themselves in an extraordinary situation—working behind enemy lines as spies.

SECRET ASIAN MEN

The secret operatives in Force 136 weren't spies in the James Bond mould. No tuxedos, Aston Martins, not even an Omega watch with a built-in laser cutter. They performed dangerous reconnaissance and sabotage missions. Among Force 136's objectives were to organize and train local underground resistance groups, intercept or disrupt Japanese communications and interfere with their supply lines. They operated similarly to MI9, or British Military Intelligence.

Britain needed Chinese Canadians who could read, write and speak Chinese so they could be placed in the Japanese-occupied countries of Burma and British Malaya, where significant portions of the populations were ethnically Chinese. Although not all of these ethnic Chinese spoke Cantonese (the dialect most Chinese Canadian agents spoke), it was believed the Chinese Canadians would blend in easily and build a better rapport with local contacts and resistance forces than the European spies.

In an article for the Burma Star Association's web page, Willie Chong, a British Columbian who served with Force 136, said the group's tasks looked like scenes out of the 1957 war movie *A Bridge Over the River Kwai* (based on a book by Pierre Boulle):

The movie…depicted the type of training these men received and the difficult task they had in hiking through thick jungle, back packing heavy loads of plastic explosives, radio transmitters and food supplies, to reach their target without being detected…They trained how to scout and how best to approach an enemy camp or ammunition dump to sabotage installations without being detected. To keep in contact with headquarters, wireless operation and Morse code training, including coding messages in a Chinese wording code system, were also a part of the course.

The men learned how to rig plastic explosives with timers and how to engage an enemy in hand-to-hand combat. They also received parachute training, on the ground and in the air. These skills were essential when it came time to drop behind enemy lines.

Alex Louie poignantly reflected on how remarkable it was that he learned to swim during his military training. As a youth in Vancouver, Louie had been a keen Boy Scout, but the public pools in the area barred Chinese Canadian Scouts from using the facilities. This segregation (whites here, Asians there) extended to restaurants and movie theatres and was reminiscent of the social divide between blacks and whites in the southern United States. Because of this, kids like Louie were never able to earn their merit badges in swimming. Years later, he finally learned to swim, but only because the army needed him to attach explosive mines to the hulls of enemy ships. He didn't earn a merit badge; he earned a licence to kill.

The training was difficult and exhausting, but it needed to be: the price these agents paid if they were discovered behind enemy lines was death, and, quite likely, a cruel and painful one. Every man was given a suicide pill and told how and when to use it. One mission was so risky that the military dubbed it "Operation Oblivion." The plan was to actually go into China in the summer of 1945 and lay the groundwork to eventually take out the Japanese troops in an all-out invasion. The Chinese Canadians recruited for that special taskforce were told the casualty rate would be nearly 80 percent.

It was essentially a suicide mission, but John Ko Bong and Alex Louie signed up for it anyway. Another man among their ranks was a Victoria man named Douglas Jung, who would later become Canada's first Chinese Canadian member of parliament. It's amazing that these men were willing to walk into near-certain death. However, as fate would have it, Operation Oblivion never took place. A few weeks before the scheduled departure date, the United States dropped an atomic bomb on the Japanese city of Hiroshima. Three days later, another bomb levelled Nagasaki. Six days after the nuclear attacks, on August 15, 1945, Japan officially surrendered to the Allies.

"When they declare[d] the war has ended, well everybody was cheering and happy and everything else," said John Ko Bong years later in an interview with Veterans Affairs Canada. "We were going to be going home, eh, but that fact that we were sent up north we were quite happy because we were going to be instrumental in receiving prisoners of war held by Japanese."

The subterfuge mission became a rescue mission, as members of Force 136 set up makeshift refugee camps for prisoners of war, mainly British soldiers. Some of these men had been locked up for three or four years, since the early days of the fighting in the Pacific. John Ko Bong recalled seeing the gaunt, emaciated figures of half-starved prisoners making their way to the camps. They were "walking like human skeletons."

"Jesus, when I saw them I said, 'Holy smoke.' All you could see was their head and the ribs, you know, skinny legs with no meat on them," said John.

During the first two weeks in September, more than 1000 tonnes of supplies, over 100 doctors and other relief workers were flown to the POW camps. The Chinese Canadians of Force 136 stayed in Southeast Asia for a little while after Japan's surrender to help oversee things until local governance was re-established. Some members even stayed until mid-November before returning to Canada.

Chinese Women in the War

It's important to also recognize the contributions of Chinese Canadian women during World War II. As with the fellas, the exact number of women who had assisted the Allies is not known. The female Chinese population in Canada was relatively small because a lot of the men who had immigrated to Canada were unable to bring their wives with them because of the head tax and the Exclusion Act. The Chinese Canadian women who were part of the war effort were born in Canada, likely second- or third-generation Canadians by then.

Overall, more than 45,000 Canadian women volunteered for military service, although they were largely trained for non-combat duty in order to free up men to fight in the field. Many Canadian women were trained as pilots and flew as part of the Women's Auxiliary Air Force. Mary Laura Wong, born in Salmon Arm, British Columbia, wanted to do the very same. "I had a dream that I should join the forces," she told Veterans Affairs Canada in an interview:

I wanted the Air Force but the Air Force had [filled] their quota of women. And I didn't want the Navy 'cause I couldn't stand black stockings in those days [laughs]. So, I joined the Army and when I went down to join the Army, the fellow [recruiter] said to me, "You're too young, you're not 18." So I said to him, "I'll be back tomorrow with my birth certificate," and he couldn't believe that I was 19.

Wong completed her basic training in Kitchener, Ontario, and was then sent to take a clerk's course. After showing immediate talent at typing, Mary Laura was asked to work as a teletype operator in Vancouver. During the war, she took dictation from the military higher-ups and relayed messages from government officials in Ottawa. She never took flight as she had hoped, but she said the experience of being part of the war effort was "wonderful." Before the war, she was a second-class citizen, forced to sit in a separate section of a movie theatre away from the whites. But during the war, she was accepted as any another Canadian. In fact, more than a few men working in the barracks were sweet on Mary Laura, occasionally bringing her Cherry Blossoms, her favourite candy.

"No, no racial discrimination of any kind," she recalled.

Other Chinese Canadian women, including John Ko Bong's sister, Mary, worked as instrument technicians, on assembly lines and in support services. Over a dozen Chinese Canadian women in Vancouver also assisted with the local St. John Ambulance Brigade and were trained in home-nursing, ambulance driving and first aid and were even taught to deliver babies. They became a remarkable all-Chinese female team known as the Women's Ambulance Corps.

When Japan surrendered, signalling the end of World War II, there was widespread relief and celebration across Canada. The Chinese Canadians who served this country during the war rejoiced as well, whether at home or stationed overseas. The end of the fighting was bittersweet for them in a way. The Chinese had stood shoulder-to-shoulder with Canadian troops, just as John Ko Bong said they would, and it seemed the racial tension had melted away for the most part. But now that the war was over, would Chinese Canadians finally gain acceptance? Would their personal sacrifices pave the way to a more optimistic future? Or would things go back to the way they were?

END OF EXCLUSION

The truth is, things didn't improve very much for Chinese Canadians, at least not right away. On the one hand, war veterans such as Alex Louie and John Ko Bong earned what they went to battle for—the right to vote, just like any other Canadian citizen. But others in the Chinese community were still denied suffrage. And despite getting the vote, Chinese Canadian veterans continued to face institutional prejudice. When they tried joining the Royal Canadian Legion, they were turned down. Thanks to support from people such as George Campbell (then the president of the Pacific veterans and father of future prime minister Kim Campbell), they eventually managed to gain a charter to form their own legion branch. These Chinese Canadian veterans wanted to take things further, though, and formed lobby groups to pressure the government to end the Exclusion Act that continued to separate so many friends and families.

For a while, it looked as though the more cynical members of the Chinese Canadian community were right—the ones who stood up in those public debates in

Vancouver as the country went to war and wondered aloud what good fighting for Canada would do. But the situation finally began to change for the Chinese in Canada, albeit slowly at first.

Several key factors helped turn the tide of public and political support for the Chinese in this country. One was that China had fought alongside the Allies during World War II, with Japan as their common enemy. It's both interesting, and saddening, to note that as the war carried on, the public image of the Chinese improved dramatically while the perception of the Japanese in Canada plummeted even further. White Canadians came to fear the Japanese and viewed Japanese Canadians with suspicion. The anti-Asian groups on the West Coast that had verbally lambasted both ethnic groups with equal ferocity focused their negative campaigns squarely on Japanese Canadians. It's difficult to say which Asian ethnicity was more severely discriminated against in Canadian history: Japanese immigrants didn't have to pay a crippling head tax like the Chinese did. On the other hand, 22,000 Chinese were never forced from their homes into internment camps for the sins of their place of origin, as Japanese Canadians were.

Another major reason why ethnic relations improved between the Chinese and white Canadians was because of a renewed international climate of peace and compassion. The events of the Holocaust had shocked and appalled the world. Over six million Jews had just been slaughtered by Nazis during World War II, victims of both radical racism and indifference to human suffering. Many countries in the West later faced criticism for not taking a more active role in rescuing persecuted Jewish people when they had the chance. During the 1930s, after the Nuremberg Laws stripped German Jews of their rights, hundreds of thousands of Jewish people saw the writing on the wall and tried to flee Europe, anticipating dark, dangerous days ahead. Boatloads of refugees arrived on North American shores, but most were turned away, sent back to their hostile continent, where many eventually ended up in the deadly concentration camps. Canada admitted only around 5000 Jewish people, one of the worst records among countries receiving refugees.

After the war, the countries involved in the League of Nations re-grouped as the United Nations, a new international organization focused on fostering cooperation between countries on economic, security and social issues. The horror of the Holocaust re-ignited many nations to dedicate themselves to promoting human rights and combating discrimination. Soon after the war concluded in 1945, every original member country, including Canada, signed the United Nations Charter, a document that included the following famous preamble:

> We the peoples of the United Nations determined: to save succeeding generations from the scourge of war, which twice in our lifetime has brought untold sorrow to mankind, and to reaffirm faith in fundamental human rights, in the dignity and worth of the human person, in the equal rights of men and women and of nations large and small, and to establish conditions under which justice and respect for the obligations arising from treaties and other sources of international law can be maintained, and to promote social progress and better standards of life in larger freedom...

As soon as Canada signed the United Nations Charter, Ottawa's discriminatory immigration policies became suddenly incompatible, something both politicians and the public noticed. It should also be noted that the United States, which had placed similar immigration bans on the Chinese over the past few decades, removed their restrictions in 1944 (though they only allowed 100 or so Chinese to immigrate each year until the mid-1960s). With the United States allowing Chinese immigration again, it became to difficult for the Canadian government to continue justifying a total ban against the Chinese.

In 1947, more than 20 years after Canada closed its doors to Chinese immigrants, the federal government repealed the Exclusion Act. In the many years since "Humiliation Day," fewer than 50 Chinese had been allowed into Canada.

So, what did this change in legislation mean for Chinese Canadians?

Well, after nearly a century of working, struggling, and building lives in this country, Chinese Canadians were finally given the right to vote in elections. British Columbia was the first province in 1947, followed by Saskatchewan, and eventually every other province lifted the various statues and regulations that restricted the rights of Chinese Canadians as citizens. Under Canada's new Citizenship Act, introduced around the same time, you could become a Canadian citizen no matter where you were born, including China.

Once again, the Chinese began arriving on Canadian shores. In 1949, over 100 Chinese immigrants were admitted to Canada, and it's heart-warming to know that nearly 70 percent of these immigrants were wives coming to rejoin their husbands after more than two decades of separation. In 1950 and 1951, around 60 percent of the Chinese immigrants were children. Entire families were finally reunited.

CHAPTER SIX

THE CHINESE AND THE MOSAIC

I mmigration picked up steadily, and by 1951, more than 2000 Chinese were being admitted into Canada each year. But despite lifting the ban, Canada continued to make it clear that white Europeans were the immigrants of choice. Canada needed immigrants to fill labour shortages during the post-war industrial boom and practically kicked the door wide open for people from the United States or Europe. In sharp contrast to the Chinese, nearly two million European immigrants were allowed to enter during the same period. The federal government maintained restrictive measures to curb mass immigration from Asian countries. Prime Minister Mackenzie King summed up Ottawa's position in the House of Commons on May 1, 1947:

> Large-scale immigration from the Orient would change the fundamental composition of the Canadian population.

Any considerable Oriental immigration would, moreover, be certain to give rise to social and economic problems of a character that might lead to serious difficulties in the field of international relations. The government, therefore, has no thought of making any change in immigration regulations which would have consequences of the kind.

I wish to state quite definitely that, apart from the repeal of the Chinese Immigration Act and the revocation of order in council P.C. 1378 of June 17, 1931, regarding naturalization, the government has no intention of removing the existing regulations respecting Asiatic immigration unless and until alternative measures of effective control have been worked out.

A key reason why so many new Chinese immigrants were the wives and children of Chinese Canadian citizens already in Canada was because the government wanted to tightly control the flow of Chinese into the country and to keep the incoming numbers as low as possible. One particularly difficult restriction for Chinese Canadians to swallow was that if any of their children in China had married or were no longer considered minors, they were not allowed in.

The events of the Cold War in the 1950s and 1960s also ushered in a fresh wave of "Sinophobia," which some politicians used to justify the tight measures against Chinese immigration. Former minister of citizenship and immigration J.W. Pickersgill tried to justify the policy in the House of Commons in 1960:

As I say, in order to make sure, particularly once the communist regime was established in China, that our limited immigration was not permitted to become an avenue for the back door infiltration of communist agents…it was felt by the government responsible at the time and has been felt by the present government since that these controls had to be maintained.

These restrictive policies led to some Chinese illegally entering Canada between the late 1940s and late 1950s. It's difficult to know exactly how many illegal Chinese immigrants came to Canada, but it was enough to prompt a government investigation in 1959. Most illegal immigrants who came forward were spared prosecution and some were allowed to stay.

Ottawa expanded its immigration admissions criteria in 1962, finally, for the first time since 1923, allowing Chinese people with no Canadian relatives to apply as independent immigrants. In 1967, the government reformed its immigration policies by introducing a universal point system, by which prospective new Canadians were assessed on the basis of education level, age, language skill in English or French and occupational demand. This change benefited the Chinese in Canada in significant ways. First, the point system applied to all potential immigrants and didn't take into account their ethnic origin, which allowed more Chinese families to reconnect. Second, the system favoured people in their prime working years.

Between 1956 and 1976, more than 50 percent of new Chinese immigrants were between the age of 15 and 34. These young Chinese Canadians helped revitalize Chinese communities around the country and began establishing a significant Chinese presence in the urban centres in eastern Canada, specifically Toronto. By the 1970s, the recently elected Pierre Trudeau and his government ushered in a whole new era of immigration reform that embraced multiculturalism and humanitarianism, all part of Trudeau's vision of Canada becoming a "just society" and a "cultural mosaic." The Immigration Act of 1976 made it easier for people of any ethnicity with family in Canada to enter the country or claim refugee status.

More than 100 years after Gold Mountain first brought a handful of Chinese to settle in Canada, after thousands came to help construct the CPR, after two world wars and following decades of discriminatory policies and racial tension, the Chinese were once again arriving in Canada in growing numbers with dreams of making new lives for themselves. But something was quite different this time around. The modern Chinese Canadians were no longer forced into a life of menial labour or confined to living and working within the ethnic enclaves of Chinatowns.

The sacrifices of the early Chinese Canadian pioneers—the ones who came from the southern provinces of mainland China and literally helped to build this country—had laid an important foundation for a new generation of Chinese Canadians. In the latter half of the 20th century, the vast majority of these new Chinese Canadians hailed from a single place: Hong Kong. This former British colony had been badly battered by World War II, but the following four decades saw this port city explode with rapid industrialization and dizzying economic growth. Many Hong Kong immigrants were well educated, knew English and had financial capital. But most importantly, these new Chinese Canadians were blessed with far more opportunities to excel in Canada than were previous Chinese immigrants. Over the next few decades, the Chinese came together and developed something absolutely remarkable and unthinkable a mere 20 years earlier: they formed a vibrant Chinese Canadian middle class integral to Canada's future.

THE THIRD WAVE

Between 1949 (two years after the federal government lifted the Exclusion Act) and 1994, it's estimated that 565,167 Chinese were admitted into Canada. This was the largest continuous flow of Chinese immigrants to date in Canadian history. The Chinese population grew from 289,245 in 1981 to 633,933 in 1991. As of 2006, about 1.2 million people in Canada were of Chinese ethnicity.

Between the 1960s and 1990s, people from Hong Kong (an island of less than 1300 square kilometres) accounted for more than two-thirds of total immigration from Chinese countries and regions, including mainland China and Taiwan. But immigration was extremely selective, especially because of the intense fear of communism that gripped the West.

These newcomers bore little resemblance to the struggling, poorly educated rural Chinese who came to Canada from Guangdong province during the gold rush and railway eras. Many new Chinese immigrants were in far better financial positions upon arriving here.

From 1954 to 1994, nearly a quarter-million people from Hong Kong immigrated to Canada. Of these individuals, 19 percent were entrepreneurs or business managers, 16 percent were professionals, such as lawyers and doctors, and 14 percent worked in sales or held office jobs. This means that about half of the Hong Kong immigrants who came to Canada during this four-decade period were urban, well-educated, white-collar types.

Growing up in a British colony also meant that many were able to converse fairly well in English. Around eight percent were in the service industry, and many of them likely intended to work in Canada's Chinese-run restaurants. Less than 10 percent were labourers, a far cry from the late 19th century, when nearly 80 percent of new Chinese immigrants worked as menial labourers in coal mines, fish canneries or laundries.

What did this mean for Canada? Well, the arrival of upwardly mobile Hong Kongers in such great numbers meant the demographics of the Chinese people in Canada and the nature of the existing Chinese communities changed dramatically. Many members of this cosmopolitan, business-oriented wave of Chinese immigrants could afford to settle in more affluent suburban areas outside of the downtown Chinese communities in Canada's major cities.

The trend continues to this day. As of 2006, a greater proportion of Chinese people live in the middle- to upper-middle class area of Richmond, a suburb of Vancouver, than in Vancouver itself. In the Greater Toronto Area (GTA), where the majority of Chinese in Canada now reside, a large number of Chinese live in townships and suburbs such as Markham and Richmond Hill, not in the downtown core.

Despite many new Chinese Canadians opting to settle outside of the cities and not in Chinatowns, Chinese enclaves tended to benefit from the influx nonetheless. The Hong Kong immigrants brought with them much more capital than their predecessors, and they helped rejuvenate Canada's Chinatowns by starting up new businesses, restaurants and Chinese-oriented services and by forming new cultural groups and political associations.

In earlier decades, Chinatowns acted as safe havens and social centres for the Chinese in Canada, but this new burst of entrepreneurial energy turned them into vital commercial areas and cultural landmarks. The Chinese Canadian community expanded across the country and prospered like few other immigration generations before them.

Because of Canada's history of restrictive immigration policies toward Asians, the early generations of Chinese Canadians were seen as sojourners or bachelor societies, since they were mostly men. The popular perception was that these immigrants were temporary Canadian residents, people looking to work hard for a few years and then return home. Politicians often cited this concept as a justification for not giving Chinese Canadians citizenship or the right to vote—many believed the Chinese in Canada weren't capable of, or even interested in, assimilating.

After the immigration reforms of the 1960s and 1970s, the ratio of male to female Chinese immigrants was far more balanced. The Chinese Canadian community was no longer viewed as a bachelor society, but issues of acceptance still remained among some non-Chinese.

An ugly public incident happened in 1979 after CTV's long-running current affairs program *W5* ran a show about the increase of Chinese Canadian university students in Canada. The piece, entitled "Campus Giveaways," used misleading statistics to suggest that Chinese students were invading Canadian universities and displacing white Canadian students. *W5* also criticized the federal government for unfairly subsidizing foreign students. The footage showed a University of Toronto pharmacy class full of young, Asian-looking students; there wasn't a white face in sight.

The program cast Chinese Canadians in a negative light and elicited a strong outcry from the Chinese Canadian community. The report didn't differentiate between students from China and actual Chinese

Canadian students—it lumped them all together and thus implied that even Canadian-born students of Chinese heritage were part of this foreign horde of scholars.

Chinese Canadians across the country mounted protests against the *W5* piece. They wrote letters to the CTV network and filed official complaints to broadcasting officials. Several other cultural advocacy groups and race activists joined in the campaigns. A few months later, more than 2500 people turned out to march from the University of Toronto to the local CTV station. It was the largest organized march in Chinese Canadian history.

CTV issued a statement of apology soon after, saying they regretted "any offense [*sic*] that may unintentionally have been given to the Chinese Canadian community."

It was an unsatisfactory response, as the network didn't acknowledge the misrepresentation of the facts. The protests and public pressure continued, until CTV's president, Murray Chercover, came forward with another, fuller apology.

> Although it was never our intention to produce a racist program, there is no doubt that the distorted statistics, combined with our visual presentation, made the program appear racist in tone and effect....We sincerely apologize for the fact that Chinese Canadians were depicted as foreigners, and for whatever distress this stereotyping may have caused them in the context of our multicultural society.

In some ways, the incident actually strengthened the Chinese Canadian community. In addition to garnering support from a multitude of other ethnic groups in Canada, the whole mess led to the formation of the Chinese Canadian National Council (CCNC) in 1980.

The CCNC has become an important voice for Chinese Canadians and works to draw attention to issues important to Canada's ethnic Chinese population. In 2005, the Toronto chapter of the CCNC was presented with an award for promoting positive race relations by the City of Toronto for its efforts in campaigning the federal government to apologize for the head tax and to provide redress to survivors.

CHAPTER SEVEN

THE HANDOVER

I mmigration to Canada from Asian countries increased steadily during the 1960s and 1970s, but an incredible surge in migration happened between the 1980s and the mid-1990s. What led so many Chinese people to leave the Pacific and seek new homes in Canada? Well, the seeds of this mass exodus had been planted several decades earlier, in the city of Hong Kong.

Hong Kong's rise from humble beginnings as a collection of fishing villages and rural farms to its current status as a skyscraper-crowded, leading global financial centre was nothing short of meteoric.

The Japanese occupation of Hong Kong during World War II had nearly destroyed the port city. The people in Hong Kong had suffered through violent oppression, massive food shortages and hyperinflation. By the time the war ended, almost half of the city's population had fled. (An interesting note: Hong Kong–born Adrienne

Clarkson, Canada's 26th Governor General, managed to escape the occupation along with her family as refugees in 1941, an extremely rare exception at the time.)

The situation looked grim for the people of Hong Kong, but after Japan's surrender in 1945, the city's population recovered rapidly. This increase happened for a few particular reasons. An ongoing and brutal ideology-based civil war in China between the Kuomintang Nationalist Party and the Communist Party led mainlanders to seek asylum in Hong Kong—as many as one million according to British reports. By 1949, when the Communists won and established the People's Republic, many big corporations from Shanghai and Guangdong followed suit to avoid contending with Chairman Mao and the new Communist authorities.

Under British rule, Hong Kong had a free market economy, and despite small Communist factions operating within the city, it enjoyed relative political stability. The sudden abundance of mainland Chinese in Hong Kong created a surplus of labour that was both skilled and cheap. The companies that migrated from China, mostly textiles and inexpensive goods manufacturers, took full advantage. The conditions were ripe for commercial expansion, and Hong Kong quickly re-invented itself as one of Asia's busiest industrial centres, becoming synonymous with cheap, mass-produced goods that included everything from umbrellas to sneakers to artificial flowers.

Hong Kong's economic development kicked into another gear during the early 1950s, after the United States slapped a trade embargo on Communist China during the Korean War. Although the conflict initially hurt Hong Kong's trade prospects, it rebounded better than basketball star Yao Ming. Hong Kong became the easiest place to obtain low-cost, high-volume goods from Asia, and the city transitioned from operating mostly as a trading post to becoming a dynamic, export-based manufacturer.

Suddenly, Hong Kong reeked of something other than the open-air fish markets and factory exhaust—it reeked of money. Construction ramped up all around town, and gleaming office towers and fancy high-rise apartment buildings began popping up everywhere. Hong Kong developers gave their housing complexes names denoting wealth and prestige, such as "Tycoon Court" or "King's Court."

It was the beginning of a radical lifestyle shift for the people in Hong Kong, and it must have been especially jarring for new immigrants accustomed to the impoverished Chinese countryside. A 1961 report by *New York Times* reporter Robert Trumbull included the following description of life in the burgeoning Asian city:

> Order is kept in a potentially turbulent population by impartial British law, yet thousands are governed by the clandestine rule of forbidden secret societies. Mansions and expensive apartments on the hillsides look onto teeming slums as well as neon crowned skyscrapers and the beautiful harbor. The world's finest automobiles, available here at bargain prices, slow down in the streets for man-drawn rickshaws that have been banned by law nearly everywhere else in the Orient. Free-spending tourists rub elbows with barefoot, destitute coolies.

Hong Kong emerged as a city of contrasts: East meets West, tradition meets innovation, poor meets rich. Investors in sharp suits sat cheek-to-jowl with factory workers in the city's *cha chaang teng*s, the modest little tea houses serving up eclectic menus of Chinese/British snacks.

The divide between the haves and have-nots only continued to grow as the region's economy glided upwards like the Victoria Peak mountain tram (one of Hong Kong's most famous attractions that offers spectacular views of the city's skyline, particularly at night).

The British colony remained the preferred place to be for Asia's Chinese populations as mainlanders experienced the social and political chaos of the Cultural Revolution between the mid-1960s and the mid-1970s. Under British governance, Hong Kongers enjoyed far more liberties than their mainland counterparts and had access to a bevy of public programs, including universal education for primary and secondary school students—crucial elements in the development of an upwardly mobile, educated class.

Hong Kong's economy shifted once again after the Cultural Revolution played out. The death of Mao Zedong in 1976 led to a change in the Communist Party's direction. Deng Xiaoping, a prominent Chinese politician who was often at loggerheads with Mao, introduced sweeping economic reforms that opened China's markets to the world and ushered in an intense period of industrialization. As manufacturing began booming in China, Hong Kong strengthened its economic ties with its former parent country, and many of the city's factory operations flowed back to the mainland to capitalize on cheaper labour.

Hong Kong emerged as one of the world's biggest centres of commercial and business services and was perceived as Asia's budding version of New York City, only with rickshaws instead of yellow taxi cabs and curb-side noodle vendors instead of hot dog stands. Along with Singapore, Taiwan and South Korea, Hong Kong was soon regarded as one of the East Asian Tigers, countries that experienced staggering economic growth and became global leaders in finance and information technology between the 1960s and 1990s.

Thousands of Hong Kong citizens began coming to Canada during this social and economic boom, my own parents included. When I was younger, I travelled to Hong Kong fairly often to visit my paternal grandparents between the 1980s and early 1990s. I revelled in the endless shopping, the monolithic air-conditioned supermalls and the abundance of delicious food. I knew people were trying to come to Canada because people talked about it a fair bit. My own grandparents were on their way to becoming permanent Canadian residents. But I wondered—why did people want to leave this amazing city after it rose from poverty and into international prominence?

The answer, my parents told me, was that no one was sure if the prosperity and liberty could possibly last.

HONG KONG RETURNS

If you remember the little history lesson in Chapter One, England assumed control of Hong Kong in 1842 at the conclusion of the First Opium War. Over the next few decades, following another Opium War, the Brits also gained (unfairly, as it were) the sovereignty of Kowloon and the New Territories. Eventually, the whole sticky mess was sorted out in a single, rather formal-sounding agreement called the Convention Between Great Britain and China Respecting an Extension of Hong Kong Territory.

Basically, after the political dust settled, Britain took out a 99-year lease on Hong Kong and its surrounding areas. The lease, signed in 1898, was set to expire in 1997.

Of course, Hong Kong was an economic gem and one of the few remaining colonies of a fading empire.

England was hard-pressed to give it up. During the early 1980s, as the handover deadline approached, Prime Minister Margaret Thatcher approached the People's Republic of China (PRC) about the possibility of maintaining a British presence or administration in Hong Kong after 1997. The mainland balked at the idea and held firm in its position that the treaty in which England gained the city and the territories was totally unfair to begin with. China, for the most part, had international support on its side.

This began a two-year negotiation period between the two countries over the heart and soul of Hong Kong. Many in Hong Kong, accustomed to civil liberties and Western-style governance, were concerned about how the handover would affect their lives. Others were somewhat more patriotic and looked forward to rejoining China. No matter where they stood, however, most Hong Kong citizens believed they should be given more input in Hong Kong's governance and affairs.

In 1984, China and Britain officially agreed to the terms of the handover. Hong Kong was allowed to maintain its semi-autonomous governance, its capitalist system and its previous way of life for the next 50 years at least. Under the "One country, two systems" principle, Hong Kong became a Special Administrative Region and was to be granted a mini-constitution, also known as the Basic Law.

This agreement may have inspired some relief among people in Hong Kong wary of the PRC's distaste for democracy and quasi-independent populations within its self-perceived borders (notably Taiwan and Tibet). But any relief was short-lived. Five years later, the entire world watched as Chinese authorities cracked down hard on their own civilians after a series of protests in

Tiananmen Square, near the famous Forbidden City in Beijing.

The death of a well-known, liberal-minded PRC official named Hu Yaobang had sparked the rallies. Some of the Communist Party's hardliners forced Hu to resign in 1987 after they became fed up with his advocacy of freedom of speech and his support of Tibetan semi-autonomy. He died of a seizure in April 1989.

Students, activists and disillusioned former PRC officials mourned Hu's passing. The entire Tiananmen Square incident began as merely a tribute to Hu, as thousands of mourners gathered to mark his death. But more and more people joined the crowds, angry with corruption in the government and calling for the democracy for which Hu had become a symbol. The protests stretched on longer and longer, week after week. It was an unprecedented display of political dissent in China and became the largest pro-democracy movement of the 20th century.

And it all came to a crashing, violent halt. In the early hours of June 4, after seven weeks of rallies and international attention, the tanks of the People's Liberation Army rolled into the square. Troops fired into the crowds, killing hundreds and wounding thousands. In the aftermath, nobody could say exactly how many people were shot and killed, crushed under vehicles or trampled to death. The Chinese government placed the number around 250, but the Chinese Red Cross put the number closer to 2000. The Red Cross later denied making that claim, a move that some international observers alleged was influenced by the authorities. The actual death toll is likely somewhere in between.

In a research paper about Hong Kong immigration to Canada, sociologist Peter Li suggested that "the confidence in Hong Kong was shaken by the events of 1989,

when China heavy-handedly suppressed the student demonstration in Tiananmen Square on June 4, 1989, and
tightened its political control in the aftermath. The
emigration exodus from Hong Kong in the early 1990s
had more to do with the military action and political
aftermath of the Tiananmen Square Incident than the
countdown towards the return of Hong Kong to China."

Hong Kong had been the biggest source of Chinese
immigration to Canada since the end of World War II.
A major reason for this was because relations with mainland China iced over during the Cold War in the 1950s.
Between 1968 and 1976, immigrants to Canada from
Hong Kong were more than twice as numerous as those
from Taiwan and mainland China combined.

During the early 1980s, the number of people emi-
grating from Hong Kong to Canada remained fairly
steady at about 8000 each year. After the British and the
PRC finalized the terms of the handover agreement in
1985, immigration numbers began to rise considerably.
Around this time, the Canadian government approved
some new measures to make the country a more favour-
able place for wealthier Chinese by expanding the policy
of admitting business or economic class immigrants to
include investors, entrepreneurs and self-employed
individuals. According to some experts, the convenient
timing of this policy change may have been made in
anticipation of a global mass migration ahead of Hong
Kong's repatriation.

Canada, with its Commonwealth connection and its
large ethnic Chinese communities, became one of the
most popular destinations. The U.S. and Australia also
experienced surges in immigration from Hong Kong.

During the late 1980s, immigration to Canada jumped
up significantly, with nearly 20,000 Hong Kong citizens

landing in Canada each year. Then Tiananmen Square happened and immigration sky-rocketed. By 1990, the number of people leaving Hong Kong reached 30,000 per year and continued to climb until immigration from Hong Kong peaked at 44,000 in 1994.

I remember, as a young child during the early 1990s, the tension and intense discussion within my own family and on Chinese language radio and television about the political upheaval in China and the impending handover. My paternal grandmother and grandfather (my *mah mah* and *yeh yeh*, as they're called in Cantonese) were coming to Canada quite frequently in a bid to obtain permanent residency, planning ahead should things go awry in Hong Kong.

The Hong Kong exodus slowed down dramatically in the mid-1990s. By this time, anyone who wanted to leave and had the financial means to do so had already left. Interestingly enough, as July 1, 1997, crept up, it appeared that many people in Hong Kong regained confidence in the post-handover future.

The repatriation date came and passed without much controversy. During the handover ceremony in Hong Kong, Britain's newly elected prime minister, Tony Blair, gave a speech, as did the colony's last governor, Chris Patten (a man affectionately dubbed "Chubby Patton" by local Chinese). Several Chinese kung-fu stars, including Jackie Chan and Jet Li, performed together in a traditional Chinese lion dance as part of the evening's events that were somehow both festive and sombre.

After the handover, the number of Hong Kong immigrants arriving in Canada continued to decline rapidly, falling from around 8000 in 1998, to 3663 in 2000 and to 1963 in 2001.

Research indicates that many of the new immigrants intended the entire time to keep one foot in Canada and one foot in Hong Kong. Hong Kong, despite the political uncertainty, had been doing extremely well economically during the early 1990s, professionals were in demand and the taxation rates were lower. Some new Chinese Canadians became "astronaut parents"—often the father or mother would work in Hong Kong while their children lived in Canada and attended school. A fair number of immigrants from Hong Kong also returned to the city fairly soon after the handover, up to 30 percent according to some estimates.

Immigration from Hong Kong to Canada since the end of the 20th century has remained relatively low. The Asian Financial Crisis, which struck around the same time as the handover, plunged Hong Kong into a recession, taking away the financial means of people looking to immigrate. Canada also adopted new tax laws in 1997 that required all Canadian residents to disclose offshore assets exceeding $100,000, which also likely discouraged business immigrants.

The dreaded political and social instability that fanned the flames of mass immigration from Hong Kong never really materialized. Hong Kong continues to operate as a capitalist society, and its people enjoy rule of law and far more civil liberties than their mainland counterparts. On Wikipedia, a pretty nifty chart offers a side-by-side comparison of what has stayed the same and what has changed since the handover. For example, English is still taught in all Hong Kong schools, and electrical plugs remain U.K. standard. However, celebrating the Queen's official birthday was done away with.

The big question still remains, though—when will Hong Kong gain universal suffrage and achieve full democracy?

The issue has been hotly debated in recent years and will certainly flare up if things aren't resolved by 2047—the end of the 50-year period the PRC promised Hong Kong that it would retain its current way of life.

As it stands, the spike in immigration to Canada during the late 1980s and early 1990s didn't affect Hong Kong itself too much. As many wealthy Hong Kong residents left, a number of mainland Chinese immigrated to Hong Kong, filling up labour shortages in most sectors. And as mainland China rode its economic growth to new heights, it soon replaced Hong Kong as Canada's primary source of immigration.

However, the effect on Canada from the Hong Kong immigration surge was immense. As we'll see in a later chapter, the newer generations of Chinese Canadians revitalized the country's struggling Chinatowns by starting restaurants and businesses and joining political associations and cultural groups. Some of Hong Kong's wealthiest business people became Canadian citizens and invested in major corporations. Victor Li, the eldest son of legendary Hong Kong billionaire Li Ka-shing, immigrated to Canada in 1983. Two decades later, Victor Li offered Air Canada $650 million to become the airline's majority shareholder. The deal eventually fell through, but it served as a clear indication of how much economic influence some Hong Kong immigrants have brought to Canada.

CHAPTER EIGHT

MANDARIN MOVES ON UP

Throughout the latter half of the 20th century, the vast majority of new Chinese Canadians arrived from Hong Kong, while a comparatively small number came from mainland China. A key reason for this situation was because between 1947, the year Canada lifted its ban on Chinese immigration, and the late 1960s, Communist China and Canada had never really established friendly diplomatic relations, largely as a result of the ideologically-based Cold War conflict. Most Western states did not formally recognize the People's Republic of China (PRC) as the country's legitimate government. They instead recognized the Republic of China (ROC) in Taiwan, led by the Kuomintang Nationalist Party that lost to the communists in the Chinese Civil War.

For more than two decades after the PRC assumed control, China largely shut itself away from the West.

Internally, the country went through a tumultuous change. Mao Zedong, the PRC's leader, introduced broad social and economic programs, such as the Great Leap Forward that aimed to transform China from a country of farmers and peasants to a modern and powerful Communist nation. The Mao-led Cultural Revolution also intended to purge China of liberal political factions and pro-capitalists. However, these policies failed disastrously, and the Chinese people suffered through widespread famine and political turmoil. Tens of millions died, from starvation or "disappeared" for political reasons, during the Mao era.

It wasn't until the early 1970s, when China split with the Soviet Union after several years of ideological divergence, that Canada and China began to form a relationship. In 1971, the Canadian government established diplomatic missions in China, while the PRC opened an embassy in Ottawa. The same year, China became a member of the United Nations, much to the displeasure of the U.S.

One year later, the two countries engaged in a sports exchange program—Canada sent ice skaters, a basketball team and badminton players over to China, and the Chinese sent over table tennis players, divers and swimmers.

In 1973, Pierre Trudeau became the first Canadian prime minister to visit Communist China, making Canada the first North American country to establish official relations with China. Trudeau, who had visited the Soviet Union two years earlier, wanted to end China's isolationism. His official visit, which was much opposed by Washington, was considered a big deal at the time, and the Chinese hosts were eager to impress Trudeau. A *Globe and Mail* report from October 11, 1973, stated:

The welcome prepared by the Chinese lived up to the occasion. A military band, an honor [sic] guard from the People's Liberation Army and about 5000 gaily dressed youngsters were on hand when the aircraft touched down....Mr. Trudeau and his wife Margaret appeared at the forward door, prompting a brief round of applause from the Chinese dignitaries.

The prime minister's visit, as well as changes in Canada's immigration system, began to encourage immigration from mainland China. Between 1968 and 1976, about 25,000 mainland Chinese immigrated to Canada, most arriving under the family class category or as refugees. Comparatively, nearly three times as many Hong Kong residents landed in Canada during the same period. People in mainland China were more likely to lack the financial resources and education level that made Hong Kongers more attractive as immigrants in the eyes of the Canadian government.

The low immigration numbers continued over the next few decades as China abandoned Mao's policies soon after the chairman's death in 1976 and began sweeping economic reforms. Under the leadership of Deng Xiaoping, a Communist Party veteran with a different economic vision than Mao, China transitioned into a market economy and rapidly grew into a manufacturing and exporting powerhouse. It wasn't capitalism—the PRC called it "socialism with Chinese characteristics." At the same time, in unison with the new economic plan and the ending isolationism, China started to ease its restrictions of Chinese citizens leaving the country.

Immigration from mainland China to Canada began picking up in the late 1980s, for two important reasons.

First, the Tiananmen Square incident in 1989 prompted the Canadian government to offer Chinese students studying in Canada the chance to apply for landed immigrant status. The violent military response in Tiananmen Square shocked Chinese people in Asia and around the world, and thousands took advantage of Canada's open door.

About 4500 mainland Chinese arrived in Canada in 1989, but in 1990, the number nearly doubled to 8116. The numbers spiked again to over 14,000 in 1991 before calming down and dropping to 10,548 the next year.

Throughout the 1990s, immigration from mainland China continued to be relatively low compared to the Hong Kong exodus, but the numbers climbed steadily each year. The second reason why immigration to Canada kicked into a higher gear was because of China's fast-growing economy.

China's economy had picked up in a big way between 1990 and 1999, as the country's gross domestic product grew about seven to eight percent annually. As part of its effort to join the World Trade Organization, China did away with most of its emigration restrictions for its citizens.

The Asian Financial Crisis in 1997, which battered Hong Kong's economy and discouraged people from immigrating to Canada, did not affect China as negatively. As a result, the number of mainland Chinese immigrating to Canada kept growing—in that year alone, over 18,000 arrived from China.

The economic reforms in China that rebooted its economy and, interestingly enough, made many people in Hong Kong rich enough to immigrate to Canada during the late 1980s and early 1990s, are now giving mainland Chinese the financial means to do the same.

Hundreds of millions of people in China have been lifted from poverty. According to the World Bank, 60 percent of China's population were living under its US$1-per-day poverty line around the time Deng Xiaoping's reforms began. As of 2004, that number had been reduced to 10 percent. By 2002, about 15 percent of China's working population had moved into the country's expanding middle class.

Members of China's new middle class tend to live in rapidly modernizing cities, such as Shanghai, Wuhan and Hangzhou, where you can find luxury hotels and Starbucks coffee. Years ago, thousands of starving, desperate Chinese left Guangdong province in the hopes of striking gold in North America.

As China's economy continues to steamroll forward (in 2007, China overtook Germany to become the world's third-largest economy and now trails only Japan and the U.S.) so does immigration to Canada. China overtook Hong Kong as the leading source of new Chinese Canadian immigrants in the late 1990s, and this trend continues today. By 2000, more than 30,000 immigrants from mainland China were arriving each year. The number had jumped to 42,000 in 2005.

The categorization of recent Chinese immigrants to Canada also reflects the burgeoning middle class in China. During the 1980s, about one-quarter to one-third of immigrants from the PRC arrived here as economic immigrants (that is, with skills and ability to contribute to our economy). That figure jumped to 57 percent in 1990. By the late 1990s, it was up to 67 percent. Since 2000, more than 80 percent of new immigrants from China are admitted under the economic class. These recent immigrants have also tended to be well educated. From 2002 to 2005, more than 40 percent of immigrants from the PRC have at least one university degree.

And more are coming. It has been an incredible turnaround for a people who were largely banned from coming to Canada less than a century ago. Until recently, Chinese Canadians were the largest visible minority group in the country, before South Asian Canadians edged past them.

Immigration from mainland China continues to trend upwards, with some analysts predicting that the number of Chinese entering Canada will rise to 60,000 annually over the next decade or so. Immigration from Hong Kong, even during the lead-up to the handover, didn't peak as high.

So how will the continued growth of the Chinese Canadian community affect Canada's future?

Toward the Future

It's hard to read a newspaper or watch TV without hearing something about the rise of China. This formerly isolated and mysterious country that many considered a potential physical threat during the Cold War is now a major economic force in the world. Some experts even believe that China will supplant the U.S. as the world's leading superpower, which is why the 21st century is already being dubbed the "Chinese Century." For people in the English-speaking world, it may be a wise idea to learn a little Mandarin, the official language of the People's Republic of China.

Canada's future and its potential is also tied to the Pacific. In 2009, Prime Minister Stephen Harper embarked on several official trips to Asia, visiting South Korea, Singapore, India and China. Canada's traditional trading partners—the U.S. and European countries—are projected to experience slow growth for quite some time. The economic pendulum has swung toward the East, and building strong trade relations with Asian countries will be essential to Canada's continued prosperity.

Canada's Chinese Canadian community, one of the largest and most successfully integrated in the Western world, will be an integral part of this country's future. Chinese immigrants are already playing a pivotal role in safeguarding this country's future by establishing homes. The natural growth rate in Canada has declined substantially since the early 1990s. In 2006, the fertility rate for Canadian women between the ages of 15 and 49 was an average of 1.5 children. A rate of 2.1 is required to merely sustain the population level. According to census data, immigration accounts for the majority of Canada's population growth. Newcomers from Asia and South Asia have propelled the tremendous urban growth in Canada, especially in the Vancouver and Toronto areas.

Bringing in working-age, educated people from overseas will be even more critical as Canada's population looks increasingly grey-haired. More than 12 percent of Canadians were 65 or older in 2001. The federal government projects the number of retirement-age Canadians will continue to increase dramatically—to nearly 15 percent in 2011, 19 percent in 2021 and about 25 percent in 2031.

The potential for the Chinese Canadian community is vast and, according to some experts, largely unrealized. In a research paper about Chinese immigration to Canada, sociologist Peter Li says that Chinese university-educated immigrants have brought significant human capital to this country. As any parent or student knows, post-secondary education costs a lot of money. Between 1996 and 2001,

Canada in theory saved itself about $1.8 billion in educational expenses by allowing more than 50,000 PRC immigrants with university degrees into the country. But during this same period, only 59 percent of them had found a job and earned any income. Li estimates that Canada lost between $226 and $354 million "from not realizing the full productivity of PRC-born university-educated immigrants."

The likely cause of all this is that Canada seems to devalue foreign credentials. But Li points out another study that found European immigrants with university degrees often earn as much as their Canadian-educated counterparts—only people of a visible minority receive lower earnings.

"Other studies have indicated that foreign accent, visible minority status and foreign credentials are often grounds for earnings devaluation," Li wrote. "It appears that [the] foreign credentials of immigrants are racialized in that the market value of foreign credentials depends in part on the racial features of the holders of [the] credentials and in part on how such features are evaluated in the Canadian market by employers."

Li suggests that Canada needs to do a better job of integrating immigrants into the workforce. Developing employment agencies to assist Canadian employers to identify Chinese Canadian immigrants with suitable credentials should be a priority, as would establishing procedures at the provincial level to help new Canadians properly assess their degrees for equivalence.

Chinese Canadian workers with multiple languages and cultural familiarity would be an invaluable resource in cultivating business and investment opportunities in Asia. And as Canada continues to transition to a knowledge-based economy, Chinese Canadians will be integral to bolstering the workforce at home. Many banks in Canada have already begun capitalizing on the immense Asian Canadian market by opening specialized branches with employees able to speak the languages of their customers.

The global economic recession of the early 21st century put things into harsh perspective for many analysts and policymakers around the world. The U.S., bruised and battered by widespread bankruptcies and a struggling housing market, needed money. By late 2009, the U.S., still technically the most powerful nation on the planet, borrowed more than $1 trillion from China, a country that was previously among the world's poorest and most unstable.

Moving forward, Canada is beginning to look past its southern neighbour and to Asian countries as keys to its economy and its future. Canadian political columnist John Ibbitson believes it would be folly to do otherwise. In a 2009 article in the *Globe and Mail*, he wrote:

> Everywhere that struggles will struggle even more with the idea of looking west rather than south or east. But everywhere that's growing, especially Canada's own bristling, cosmopolitan cities, will embrace Pacific Canada. They will know that the future is Asian, and the possibilities are endless.

Chapter Nine

CHINATOWNS IN WESTERN CANADA

As a child, I vividly remember the occasions my father drove our family down to Toronto and took us to the city's main Chinatown. Like many Chinese families who settled in Canada after the 1960s, we lived outside the city in a quiet suburb. The drive typically took just under an hour on the weekends, but my sister and I usually nodded off 15 minutes into the ride, as the car's steady vibrations and the radio's soft pop songs worked better than a mug of warm milk to put us to sleep.

I'd always begin to stir just as my dad took the Spadina Avenue exit off the expressway. As I'd rub the sleep from my eyes, I'd look out the window and notice that the two-storey houses and manicured green lawns of the suburbs had morphed into old Victorian buildings, giant billboards and streets just absolutely teeming with people. While my dad drove along Spadina Avenue,

I'd notice that the faces became increasingly Asian-looking, and the street signs featured Chinese characters as well as English.

My dad would eventually park the car (anywhere he could, frankly) and usher us onto *tong yun gai*—literally, in Cantonese, "Chinese people's street." Chinatown, I was told, was where we came for the really good, authentic Chinese food we couldn't get in our area. I'd take my mom's hand and walk past the bustling fruit markets, careful to avoid bumping into passing pedestrians and listening intently to the snippets of different Chinese dialects floating through the air—Cantonese, Shanghainese, Mandarin, all sounding exotic yet familiar at the same time.

Sometimes, I'd sample strange-looking fruits imported from Asia at these market stands. You merely had to point at the object of your interest and a man with cloth gloves and an X-Acto blade (who also usually had a cigarette dangling precariously from his lips) would slice off a piece for you to try. Sweet lychee or *longan* dragon eyes. Yellow and pulpy jackfruit. I'd see the intimidating-looking durian fruit, a notoriously foul-smelling item easily recognized by its porcupine-like spiked skin, cocooned in plastic and hung from posts. Unlike most supermarkets I had been in, people were encouraged, if not expected, to just reach in and sample the goods.

Beside the fruit stands were other street hawkers, often grey-haired Chinese women selling cheap, colourful clothes and handbags, sometimes stitched with names resembling famous designers and brands such as "Guchi" instead of Gucci or "Rebook" rather than Reebok. I owned a small collection of bizarre T-shirts that somehow featured the stitched images of both the popular comic characters Calvin and Hobbes *and* the Nike swoosh. Some stores competed for space on the streets by putting out display tables laden with everything from no-name electronic parts to slightly dented tin woks.

We usually took a quick browse, but before long, our stomachs collectively growled and we would scour the streets for a meal. Perhaps in a small, steamy noodle shop or one of those barbecue joints where they hang roasted ducks and chickens, auburn-coloured and glistening, in the front windows.

If we weren't in Chinatown for food, we were there to see the latest Chinese language movies. I remember watching early Jet Li kung-fu movies imported from China, when he was still largely unknown to Hollywood. During the summer, my family and I would sometimes stumble upon a street festival, and I'd stare wide-eyed at the colourful, memorizing lion dancers.

Later in my life, I'd have the opportunity to visit Chinatowns in other parts of the country. I wandered around Vancouver's Chinatown, tasting the freshest, most delicious stir-fried crab in their restaurants, and enjoying moments of quiet reflection in the beautiful Dr. Sun Yat Sen Classical Chinese Garden. Other family trips took us to Chinatown's in Montreal, Ottawa and Winnipeg. I've also travelled to some of the most historic Chinatowns in the United States, including those in San Francisco and New York. Everywhere I went, I saw people of all ethnic backgrounds walking the streets of Chinatown.

For many Canadians, this is the typical Chinatown experience—food, fun and consumerism. In the 21st century, Chinatown has become a place where people can sample delicious cuisine, hunt for bargains and explore Chinese culture in all its diverse, unique glory. For recent Chinese immigrants, like my parents, Chinatown is a place to reconnect with their original home and to be among people who grew up speaking similar languages and sharing similar values.

But for the first Chinese Canadians, the ones who arrived in Canada way back in the day, Chinatowns were so much more than commercial and cultural centres. They were lifelines. They provided a haven for new Chinese immigrants who were treated with suspicion and contempt by white Canadians during the early years of this country's history. And although there was life and spirit and verve in the streets back then, like there is today, there was also darkness, despair and a lot of loneliness. Chinatown was a source of comfort and strength, and it was a place that fostered the growth of Chinese associations and activist movements that pushed for equal rights and fair treatment.

The term "Chinatown" is a pretty loose definition that was used to describe any section of a city occupied by Chinese people. During the 19th century, North American coastal cities such as San Francisco, Victoria and Vancouver acted as the major landing pads for workers shipping in from China. After clusters of immigrants had arrived in these cities, they took up residence on one or two streets, rarely leaving this tiny sector except for work. As stated earlier, the Chinese called it the "Chinese people's street," while the local English-speaking population referred to it as "Chinamen's quarters" or "Chinatown."

The first Chinese settlements in British Columbia emerged after gold was found along the Fraser River, and contingents of Chinese miners who had been digging in California and Washington followed the rush up north. Previous mining experiences had taught them to stick together. The European men had never been keen on sharing their mines and space, and they treated the Chinese with hostility. Bloody brawls weren't uncommon.

Back in those days, there were two types of Chinatowns. There were spontaneous or "instant" Chinatowns that essentially were a collection of improvised shacks set up in small mining settlements in the valleys throughout the expansive wilderness of what is now termed the Cariboo Chilcotin Coast. These makeshift communities didn't have any real institutions or permanent fixtures, and most of the temporary homes were left to rot away after their inhabitants moved on.

The other kind of Chinatown, of a more permanent nature, was established in British Columbia's large mining towns and in cities such as Yale and Barkerville. Victoria, however, has the honour of being home to Canada's oldest extant Chinatown.

VICTORIA: THE FIRST CHINATOWN

Because most of the Chinese in Canada between the mid-19th century and the mid-20th century lived in British Columbia, it's no surprise that Victoria had the country's most populated Chinatown for 50 years. The city's Chinatown remains one of the most historically significant places in Canada and has been officially designated a National Historic Site.

In 1843, the Hudson's Bay Company built a fur-trading post at what is now Victoria to service the New Caledonia area (now mainland British Columbia). By the time the Chinese began arriving for the gold rush of 1858, other ethnic groups had already settled in many sections of Victoria. British professionals, such as doctors and lawyers, tended to live on the city's hillsides, while former Hudson's Bay Company employees and Jewish merchants took up other streets. The local Songhees Natives resided in a village in Victoria's inner harbour. The Chinese set up shop on the city's northern fringe, near the ravine, and were largely forced to live out of tents or shacks on mudflats.

But Victoria was booming, which attracted more Chinese miners, merchants and money. Already in 1858, a Chinese business owner named Chang Tsoo arrived in the city. Chang, who had a lot of connections in San Francisco, encouraged more Chinese people to come, and he helped them settle by organizing housing, food, clothes and mining equipment.

Other Chinese-run companies came into the mix, too. Lee Chong and the Loo brothers brought in the Kwong Lee Company, a San Francisco–based firm that operated general supplies stores. In fact, Mr. Lee's wife had the distinction of being the first Chinese woman to land in Canada when she arrived in Victoria in 1860. Another big company was Tai Soong. Eventually, several of these Chinese merchants bought most of the real estate Chinatown was situated on. Real buildings and stores replaced the shacks.

By 1862, Victoria's Chinese population numbered around 300. Nearly all the residents of Chinatown were men who worked as tailors or cobblers or provided other services for the miners. Some other Chinese lived out-side the immediate Chinatown block, in farms or stores or, if they worked as domestic help or personal cooks, in the houses of their well-to-do employers.

As the gold rush continued, the Chinese population gradually increased. Chinese companies began import-ing food products and distributing them to other parts of the province through branch stores. These stores often collected money from the Chinese workers and sent it back to China for them. The store employees also received mail for the workers and read it out to them if they weren't able to read Chinese.

Chinatown's population fluctuated depending on the time of year. During winter and spring, Chinatown was full of miners or builders who drifted back when the weather got too cold or too wet to pan for gold or construct trails and wagon roads.

The residents of Chinatown had an uneasy co-existence with their white neighbours. Early on, few non-Chinese ventured into the ethnic enclave. Most Canadians believed the Chinese were intellectually inferior, culturally backward and unable to integrate into mainstream society. What could they possibly offer the rest of Canada besides their affordable, efficient labour? Chinatown was considered to have the social standing of a red-light district, a place where no man or woman of upstanding moral character would dare enter.

As it was, Chinatown was a community of bachelors, which resulted in some particular social problems. Information from this time period indicates many of the Chinese workers were married men, even if they had only been wed for a few weeks before setting sail for North America. The gender ratio in Victoria's Chinatown during the late 1870s, for example, was often well over 200 men for every woman. There was more testosterone filling the air in Chinatown than in the backstage area of a men's weightlifting competition.

In an effort to cope with the terrible loneliness, some of the men spent their hard-earned money on female company. Prostitution quickly became a common vice in Chinatown, and by the late 1800s, men could choose from nine different local brothels.

Gambling was another popular pastime. Chinese men slipped into the semi-hidden gambling dens along the dark, narrow alleyways. One of the most common betting games from China was fan-tan, a type of Chinese roulette. Victoria's Chinatown features a Fan Tan Alley that, at less than one metre wide, has the honour of being one of the narrowest alleyways in Canada. Another favourite Chinese game was mah-jong, the multi-player tile game that later become popular with many Westerners, especially, it seems, for older Jewish women.

Drug use was also a big problem in the Chinese quarter, as opium was still fashionable at the time, and dangerously addictive. Crude opium, grown in India, was exported to Hong Kong and then shipped to North America. For a long time, manufacturing and selling opium was the biggest business in Victoria's Chinatown, even though the authorities levied a tax of $100 against Chinese merchants selling the drug, while white pharmacists were left alone. In Victoria, Kwong Lee and Tai Soong were the largest opium dealers in Chinatown. Behind their main stores, workers cooked up batches of opium in boiling water for several hours until they formed into a jelly-like substance. The drugs were then canned and sold. Victoria became one of the largest opium distribution points on the continent, until the federal government made the drug illegal in 1908.

The debauchery of many of the Chinese menfolk certainly didn't do much to win the hearts of white Canadians. And their carrying-out of likely unsanitary activities (such as feeding pigs on the town streets), which were considered acceptable in their native country, added to the overwhelmingly negative perception of Chinatown.

A clergyman who had been working with some of the Chinese and Japanese immigrants in British Columbia described Chinatown as:

...a miniature Chinese town built by Chinese carpenters, without any regard for beauty, regularity, sanitation or comfort; a segregated group of individuals who realized that they were unloved and separated from their neighbours by an almost impassable gulf of race, colour, language and thought... Within the unshapely structures of Chinatown were the parasites of the Chinese race—professional gamblers, opium eaters, and men of impurity... Chinatown became the carcass to attract the foul birds of Western vices, the dumping ground of those evils which the white man wishes removed from his own door.

Not all Chinese people were seen as filthy, whoring drug addicts. Some of the wealthy, influential merchants, most notably Lee Chong of the Kwong Lee Company, were well respected by the white political and business communities. Chong merited several positive mentions in local newspapers over the years.

Victoria's Chinatown was established during the mid-19th century gold rush and is the oldest in Canada.

In the 1850s, the Chinatown in Victoria was mostly a collection of wooden shacks and tents inhabited by Chinese men who worked as miners or labourers.

During the 1880s, the Chinese population in Victoria continued to increase as the construction of the national railway brought tens of thousands of new immigrants to the city. Because of the lack of housing, newcomers often slept on the floors of crowded cabins. Chinatown did not have sidewalks, sewers or running water.

By this time, some Chinese Canadians were learning English at the Methodist mission, but the tutoring was usually accompanied by a conversion of faith. Interaction between the Chinese and non-Chinese in Victoria was increasing, but not always for benign reasons.

Racism was on the rise after the gold deposits were cleaned out and railway jobs dried up. Canada fell in and out of recessions. Victoria's white labour groups continually lobbied the government to block Chinese immigration because they considered the Chinese to be undercutting them in the competition for jobs by working for less money. The provincial government made a few attempts to tax Chinese workers and exclude them from certain jobs, but the merchants of Chinatown used their relatively impressive sway to convince the federal government to thwart these efforts.

Still, a climate of hostility permeated Chinatown. Not only were the Chinese battling with white Canadians, but they were also fighting each other. Throngs of unemployed, angry Chinese immigrants got into fights with Chinese Canadians already settled in Victoria. Regional and clan loyalties, which were very important in China, definitely played a part in these disputes.

In 1884, several merchants got together and formed the Chinese Consolidated Benevolent Association (CCBA). Similar community groups already existed in the U.S. The association informed the Chinese Consul-General how "gangs of vicious Chinese were bullying their fellow countrymen; the old, the poor and the unemployed suffered from coldness, sickness, and starvation, and some had died in the streets; prostitution, gambling, brawling, fighting, intimidation and extortion pervaded the Chinese communities."

The CCBA became the first collective Chinese voice in Canada. The association fought against discriminatory laws and established rules of conduct for the Chinese. A Chinese person harassed or abused by a Westerner could go to the CCBA for help. Chinese girls who were sold into slavery or marriage in Victoria were rescued and turned over to the group and sent to Hong Kong. If a Chinese person was so impoverished he could no longer live in Canada, the CCBA arranged for him to return to China. For those Chinese who died, the association maintained a cemetery or held onto their remains so they could be shipped back home one day.

Thanks to punishing recessions in the late 19th century, the economy and racial hostility got so bad in British Columbia that the CCBA wrote to China advising people *not* to come to Canada. It was estimated that the cost of living in the country was 10 times greater than it was in China. "If you...are determined to come, you should bring along with you some extra money...to pay for your board and lodging while you are still seeking work. Otherwise, you will find yourself in a terrible plight and have to sleep in the open with no job, no food, and no salvation."

The CCBA also helped out in schooling for Chinese Canadian children. In 1899, the association built a Chinese school. But a few years later, its lawyers got involved after some local white Canadians began a movement calling for the segregation of Chinese students in Victoria's schools. In 1903, Victoria School Board became the only one in the country to separate Chinese students from their white classmates.

Chinese parents were furious at this act of discrimination. They had for years already had to endure their children being attacked by white children. Schoolgirls often complained of being pelted with rocks or being pushed to the ground by boys. A Chinese boy actually lost his leg when, as he tried to flee a small mob of white school kids, he ran into the path of a streetcar. In court, the attackers' parents agreed to pay $250 in damages. They didn't follow through, and when the Chinese parents took them to court again, the judge acquitted the attackers.

The *Colonist* newspaper even showed sympathy when it reported another terrible incident in 1899:

On Sunday afternoon...a little Chinese boy, carrying a school bag containing some fruit...was assaulted by several large boys at the corner of Johnson and Blanchard streets. He was most unmercifully beaten and the bag and its contents thrown into the mud and destroyed. Two men standing near did not interfere, but looked calmly on at the cowardly act....The police were notified, but nothing further has been heard about it.

As the years went on, the issue of fair treatment continued to pull various Chinese organizations and sympathetic whites together. The federal government had permitted a head tax refund for Chinese immigrant children provided they attended an English-speaking school for at least one year. Not many Chinese families took advantage of this offer, until 1903, when the head tax rose from $100 per person to $500—astronomical at the time. At this point, Victoria's school board barred many Chinese children from attending classes, arguing that the children lacked enough basic English to succeed academically. It would just be a waste of dollars.

The Chinese Consolidated Benevolent Association's lawyers countered this discriminatory action by contending that many French Canadian children had similarly limited ability in English but they weren't denied an education. The arguments didn't change the school board's position, however. Partial segregation continued in Victoria, as the school board later decided to bar any Chinese child over the age of 10 from attending classes because such children were suspected of going to school just to gain the tax refund.

As the Chinese continued to fight against discrimination, events back in the homeland increasingly caused tension in Victoria. China began the 20th century in utter turmoil. The Qing Dynasty was overthrown by a republican revolution leading to the formation of the Republic of China (ROC). What followed were decades of civil war between the Kuomintang Nationalist Party, the ROC's leading party, and the Communist Party. The various allegiances and political loyalties travelled across the seas and found their way into Victoria's Chinatown.

By 1910, about 3500 Chinese people were living in Victoria. Many of them were part of political and community organizations. A Chinese Freemason's branch had already been around for some time. Canadian-born Chinese men, now coming of age, formed different groups, from social advocacy ones, such as the Chinese Young Men's Progress Party, to athletic clubs and football teams. Incidents of violence occurred on occasion, with one notable dust-up between the Freemasons and Kuomintang supporters in 1928 after an argument ignited over funding for the CCBA and a local Chinatown library. Still, Victoria's Chinese population was united when it came to one issue: the Japanese invasion of China in the early 1930s. The CCBA started a group called "Resist Japan and Save the Nation" and was able to raise huge amounts of money—$20,000 in one particular year—to help support troops in China. As the Sino-Japanese war deepened, Chinatown rallies became increasingly ugly. There were reported incidents of people throwing themselves in front of trucks shipping iron destined for Japan.

As mentioned earlier, the turning point for the Chinese in Canada largely came during World War II when Canada and China became allies and Japan became the common enemy. The wartime efforts of Chinese Canadians, especially in Victoria's Chinatown, helped create lasting bridges of goodwill and national unity.

The Chinatown community groups, already accustomed to pooling resources and collecting funds, went into overdrive. The Chinatown residents gave generously. Victoria's Chinese population, a mere few thousand people, raised $750,000 for China's war effort against Japan. And despite representing less than 10 percent of Canada's entire Chinese population, they bought 20 percent of all war bond purchases. The federal government publicly thanked them over and over. Victoria's Chinese families contributed more than money. Many of their children offered to enlist for military service. Several members of the special operations group Force 136 hailed from Victoria.

The treatment of Chinese Canadians after the war improved gradually, but, unfortunately, Victoria's Chinatown slipped into a period of decline. The population shrank as Chinese people moved freely through Canada and new immigrants chose to settle in bigger metropolitan areas. Many of the Chinese businesses and associations that had fuelled the early growth of Chinatown folded. By 1951, fewer than 2000 people lived there, the lowest number in 60 years. Throughout the 1960s and 1970s, the buildings in Victoria's Chinatown crumbled, and while its population increased with changes in immigration policy, it couldn't keep pace with the Chinatowns in Vancouver, Toronto and Calgary.

A series of plans were introduced around 1979 to reinvigorate Victoria's Chinatown by beautifying its streets and promoting Chinese business and trade. In 1997, there was even a proposal to start a Chinese-themed casino, although many residents opposed it out of fear it would contribute to the stereotype that Chinese people are degenerate gamblers. The anti-casino movement won out.

While the renewal efforts certainly helped to preserve the historical significance of Chinatown, they failed to attract new residents. By 2001, fewer than 12,000 Chinese people lived there, which made Victoria's Chinatown, once the largest in the country, now one of the smallest. The recent immigration booms from Hong Kong and China largely skipped Victoria—in fact, more than 40 percent of the Chinese currently living in this Chinatown are Canadian-born.

The new Chinese Canadians gravitated toward the suburban areas of two of Canada's most populous metropolitan areas—Vancouver and Toronto. But Victoria's Chinatown played a crucial role in the early years of Chinese immigration to Canada. As the very first established Chinatown, it provided a template for community and connection among Chinese Canadians. It may be one of the quietest and least populated Chinatowns in Canada today, but it remains an important part of Chinese Canadian history.

Of course, Victoria isn't the only significant Chinatown in this country. Each is somehow unique. Some cities, such as Toronto, have more than one Chinatown, and each Chinatown in Canada has experienced periods of growth, decline and revitalization. Let's take a quick look at the history of some other Chinatowns, from west to east.

VANCOUVER

If Victoria's Chinatown led the way up until the end of World War II, then Vancouver's Chinatown leapfrogged over it afterward. The Chinese settled in Vancouver shortly after the rise of Victoria's Chinatown. The Vancouver Chinese community was mostly composed of fish cannery workers and former railway employees, which most likely explains why Chinatown was situated near the harbour docks, in close proximity to the railway lines and commercial district.

The city's population grew rapidly during the early 20th century, quadrupling to 120,000 between 1901 and 1911. Vancouver's Chinese population increased as well, with about 3600 ethnic Chinese at this point, making it the largest Chinese community in the country, just slightly larger than Victoria's Chinese population. They formed groups such as the Chinese Benevolent Association (CBA), which ran a hospital and helped to equip a playground for children. Some Chinese studied English through Christian-run schools. As the years passed, Chinese entertainment became more widely available. Traditional Chinese opera, with its elaborate, colourful costumes, haunted-sounding singing and exciting acrobatic flair, was a popular escape for Vancouver's Chinese.

The Chinese in Vancouver faced tough times, like all the other Chinese across Canada, socially and economically. Racial hostility led to the 1907 riots in Chinatown. A few years later, a recession battered the British Columbian economy, leaving up to 80 percent of Vancouver's Chinese without jobs. The Chinese got by the best they could, most working as grocers, farmers, fish canners and shingle makers. As you can imagine, the rampant poverty in the province only fanned the flames of racial tension. The Chinese were routinely subject to arbitrary licensing fees and regulations. Chinese restaurant owners were also barred from hiring white waitresses.

However, the difficult times actually worked to facilitate some common ground between Chinese and white workers. In 1917, many of Vancouver's Chinese factory workers and their white colleagues formed unions. Because nearly 70 percent of the workforce were

Chinese, the factories in Vancouver and New Westminster were forced to shut down when they went on strike.

The Depression of the 1930s struck Vancouver hard, and some in the Chinese community needed to beg on the streets to survive. The government gave out relief money, but the Chinese always received less than white Canadians. Things were so bad that the Chinese associations, their resources already stretched thin, began sending some of the poorest back to China, because a boat ticket was more affordable than supporting them.

After World War II, many Chinese had earned the right to vote, but the discriminatory immigration ban still separated many families. The Chinese associations in Vancouver lobbied the federal government hard on this issue. The CBA's chairman, Wong Foon Sien, went to Ottawa 11 times. Sien was lobbying on behalf of a Chinese man named Leong Hung Hing, whose son by his second wife in China had been refused entry into Canada.

Leong had the support of the province's and country's respective supreme courts, but the federal government passed legislation prohibiting this kind of immigration sponsorship. Not long after the supreme courts' rulings, the man passed away.

"I believe most of the immigration officials have families," Wong Foon Sien wrote to the federal government:

> Their children on Christmas morning will sit on their fathers' knees and gleefully open parcels...I cannot help but think about Leong Hung Hing's little boy who will certainly have no parcels to open on this day. He would not hear again the words of encouragement from his...father whom he was unable to join and whom he will never see. He is wondering where his father [is] buried and will he be

permitted to gather some daisies to put on the grave in the spring and autumn as dutiful sons should do.

Canada eventually relaxed its immigration laws and embraced a more multicultural approach. In the 1950s, Vancouver's Chinese population shot up from 8700 to 15,000, after the Chinese immigration ban was lifted, and wives and children came, reuniting long-lost families. In the 1970s, wealthier Chinese, mostly from Hong Kong and Taiwan, came to Vancouver and rejuvenated the Chinese Canadian community through investments. Stores, cafes and restaurants multiplied, causing Chinatown to expand its borders. Land prices went up dramatically, and the influx of capital helped modernize Chinatown, but tensions mounted between the new immigrants and older Chinese Canadians. Socioeconomic class and status became an issue. Some Chinese Canadian youth, who perhaps struggled academically because of their limited English, became involved in street gangs.

During these decades, relations between Vancouver's Chinese community and other Canadians improved. The stores, cuisine and festivals attracted many non-Chinese to Chinatown. The city's Canadian-born Chinese were also well integrated into mainstream society.

But the tidal wave of Chinese immigration from Hong Kong in the 1980s and 1990s prompted another wave of ethnic friction. Between 1986 and 2001, Vancouver incorporated 214,000 Chinese immigrants into the mix. During the late 1980s, house prices rose significantly on the city's west side, and the blame was placed squarely on new Chinese immigrants, specifically the wealthy ones from Hong Kong. News stories decried how new Chinese Canadians were building monster homes and cutting down mature trees.

Ironically, the Chinese population surge led to the decline of the city's Chinatown. New Chinese commercial districts, such as The Golden Village in the suburb of Richmond, have become more popular destinations for the area's Chinese Canadians. Chinatown's advocacy groups opened up satellite offices in the suburbs, making Chinatown less of a central point of organization. The province also designated the Vancouver's Chinatown a heritage site, which was a lovely recognition, but it limited development and renovations.

Nevertheless, Vancouver's Chinatown remains the second largest Chinatown in North America, in area, after San Francisco. It may no longer be the primary community for Vancouver's Chinese population, but Chinatown should be remembered and respected for fostering generations of Chinese Canadian activists, politicians, artists and upstanding citizens who helped shape the bright future of Canada's Chinese.

CALGARY

Before the 1880s, you couldn't find a Chinatown outside British Columbia. According to data from 1881, there were only 10 Chinese in Toronto, eight in the Barrie region and seven in Montréal. Smaller cities such as Winnipeg and Hamilton had maybe one or two Chinese residents. Travelling between provinces was difficult because of the enormous barrier of the Rocky Mountains and the vast distances. The Canada Pacific Railway would soon change everything, however.

The construction of the national railway brought many Chinese into the Alberta region. Most Chinese in Calgary, Edmonton and Lethbridge made their living selling vegetables or running cafes and laundries. Others had jobs in sugar factories or mined coal near the town of Banff. Calgary's first Chinatown was established in the northeastern part of the town's centre. There were several eateries, one tailor, one grocer and a few laundries.

In June 1892, a Chinese man who had just returned from Vancouver contracted small pox. The city's officials burned the laundry where he was staying and quarantined four other Chinese men who lived outside of town. Nine people ended up contracting small pox, with three of them dying.

Some months later, the Chinese men were released from quarantine but were met with an angry mob. About 300 men, who blamed the Chinese for bringing small pox into the town, attacked the Chinese stores, smashing windows and trying to start fires. Many Chinese fled the scene, taking refuge with church officials or at the police barracks. It took weeks for things to calm back down.

By 1900, there were over 60 Chinese people in Calgary. Many of them wanted to learn English but were turned away by the local Presbyterian church, after members of its congregation objected. Instead, a man named Thomas Underwood, a Baptist who had become acquainted with the Chinese during the railway years, kindly offered to put up a two-room building where they could take classes. When that building became too small, a larger one, called the "Chinese Mission," was erected. As the city's Chinese population grew, a second Chinatown formed around this structure.

Calgary's second Chinatown didn't last long, though. As more white settlers and farmers arrived, the city decided to build a hotel and vehicle depot downtown, which caused the value of land near this Chinatown to go up considerably in value. The Chinese, who were renting at this point, were evicted without hesitation.

Calgary's Chinese residents take part in a parade in 1905. The completion of the CPR in the late 19th century saw more Chinese migrate eastward from BC.

⸺⊶⊷⸻

The Chinese merchants purchased land around Centre Street and Second Avenue Southeast with the intention of establishing a third Chinatown. The move was met with a lot of resistance. Property owners near the proposed site were infuriated and concerned that land values would drop if the Chinese moved in. The *Calgary Herald* agreed with the protesters. In an editorial from 1910, the newspaper stated that if the third Chinatown went ahead, then "white people will be glad to sell out and Chinese will be glad to buy at cheap prices. Thus, like a festering sore their presence will spread from block to block to their own profit and the city's detriment."

A festering sore? Ouch.

Not everyone in the Calgary establishment suffered from a case of Sinophobia, though. The local officials, including the medical health officer and police chief, were in favour of the Chinese. They gave the green light to the third, and final, Calgary Chinatown.

By 1915, there were about 100 Chinese grocery stores, cafes, restaurants and laundries. As in Victoria and Vancouver and other Chinatowns across Canada, the Chinese community in Calgary formed associations and community groups. They also imported political loyalties that sometimes led to violent feuds.

The Chinese came together when it came to combatting discrimination, though. Throughout the 1930s, when the Depression ravaged most of the world's countries, jobless Chinese received $1.12 each week in relief money while a white person received $2.50. The Chinese organized rallies and picketed outside government offices and Calgary City Hall. In January 1937, several Chinese protested the unfair relief rates by holding sit-downs on the city's streetcar tracks. That was certainly one way to get people's attention. The efforts eventually paid off, as the provincial government raised the rate for the Chinese to $2.12.

The Calgary Chinese also united, as in Victoria and Vancouver and other Canadian Chinatowns, when it came to raising funds for the war efforts, especially World War II. Calgary's Chinese community raised over $200,000 for China between 1937 and 1945.

The Chinese in Calgary became involved very early on in industries particular to the province. Many worked for cattle ranchers, often as cooks or farm hands. After World War II concluded and immigration laws changed, Chinese immigrants joined their relatives in Calgary and often found work in the oil industry. The city's Chinese population, which had dipped between the world wars, experienced an upswing during the 1950s and 1960s.

Part of this growth came from the arrival of 250 mail-order brides, as single Chinese men looked to settle down but lacked suitable Chinese female partners. Vivienne Poy, who became the first Chinese Canadian senator in 1998, wrote her academic dissertation on Chinese immigrant women. Poy interviewed several Chinese mail-order brides and sadly found that some had come from unfortunate circumstances in China and were abused by their new husbands. One such woman had two children from a previous marriage and had admitted suffering domestic abuse, but she said she was still grateful to the man who brought her to Canada.

"Landed immigrant status was worth all the abuse she had to suffer," Poy said at a discussion for the Women's Legal Education and Action Fund in 2005. "Besides, 'saving face' is very important in the Chinese culture, and one does not hang one's dirty laundry out in public. So, getting help from outside of one's family was out of the question."

As the decades moved on, the Chinese became more integrated with mainstream Canadian society, and several Canadian-born Chinese Calgarians became popular mainstream public figures. Normie Kwong earned the distinction of being the first Chinese Canadian to play in the Canadian Football League when he suited up for the Stampeders in 1948 (more on him in the upcoming sports chapter). Kwong, who was nicknamed "China Clipper," helped the Stampeders win the Grey Cup in his rookie season. He later won three more championships with the Edmonton Eskimos.

In 1958, a reputed local beauty named Jennie Chow was crowned Queen of the Calgary Stampede. She had been chosen as a nominee by the Calgary Fire Department, and the Chinese community rallied behind her. "I'm very proud of my community and I hope they're proud of me," she told CBC Radio after her win. "There's not too many Chinese in Calgary, but I just think they're really wonderful." If you close your eyes when you listen to that radio clip, you'd be unable to tell she was Chinese. Fresh from her Stampede win, Chow sounded like any other young Calgary gal.

Land redevelopment in the 1980s threatened Calgary's Chinatown as some developers proposed adding sky-scrapers and urbanizing the area. Members of the Chinese community and the city council agreed that this would change the nature of Chinatown, and they formulated a new plan to help preserve the historic site as much as possible. Part of this new plan included the construction of a spectacular Chinese cultural building, a place where the Chinese community could celebrate and preserve their culture.

Opened in 1992, Calgary's Chinese Cultural Centre (CCC) is a beautiful building modelled after the Taoist-style structures in the Hall of Prayers and the Temple of Heaven in Beijing. The CCC features a dome covered in tiles imported from China, made by the same company that helped decorate the Temple of Heaven during the Ming Dynasty.

But Calgary's Chinese community, as it had for several decades, took great efforts to engage with the city's broader population. So, in addition to hosting Chinese cultural events, the CCC holds many other activities, such as political meetings, citizenship ceremonies, Calgary Philharmonic Orchestra performances and art exhibitions.

The next wave of Chinese immigration brought to Calgary a major influx of Chinese, some of whom preferred the city to Vancouver or Toronto because it was less busy, with a relatively low crime rate and more reasonable housing prices. An estimated 130 Hong Kong entrepreneurs brought over businesses or invested in firms, creating 400 full-time jobs in Calgary between 1996 and 1999. By the 21st century, Calgary was home to the fourth-largest Chinese community in Canada. About one-third of the city's Chinese population were Canadian-born and nearly half had arrived during the 1990s. Calgary's Chinatown is now the third largest in Canada, after those in Vancouver and Toronto.

WINNIPEG

The first Chinese arrived in Winnipeg in 1877, lured there because more job prospects were available to them here than in cities farther west. The city's overall population stood at about 2000, and many of the Chinese workers started laundries to serve the residents.

By 1890, more than ten Chinese-run laundries operated in the city. Immigrants with the surname Lee came to dominate the city's early laundry industry. The Lees stuck together and cut prices against other competitors. They even blocked Chinese newcomers from entering the city by ganging up on them at the railway station, beating them up and then forcing them back onto the train. Eventually, Lee clan representatives from British Columbia came to Winnipeg to help smooth things over with the other Chinese clans in the city. Winnipeg's Chinese population grew slowly.

In 1901, there were about 100 Chinese working in 29 laundries around the city. The first Chinese shop, Quong Chong Tai, opened in 1905 on King Street. The city's Chinatown developed along the street as well. By 1920, there were 900 Chinese living in Winnipeg, including eight families. At this time, there were

150 laundries, a few Chinese restaurants and several Chinese grocery stores.

As the city's Chinatown expanded, health inspectors often took Chinese landlords to court for overcrowding their boarding houses. The Chinese in Winnipeg largely kept to themselves. Like elsewhere, they formed political associations and clan organizations. The early 1920s saw dramatic art clubs like the Jing Hun She added into the mix. As many as 30 members would come together to sing and play musical instruments. The group performed Chinese operas and screened Chinese films at a local theatre.

One elderly Chinese later reflected on how important those plays and movies were to the community:

> We knew the stories by heart. They gave us some life, something to make us laugh and cry, to do something other than work. We were not allowed in the white man's cinema then you know, nor at social gatherings. Nothing for Chinese. We were totally separated from white people, except for doing business.

As the Depression gripped Canada throughout the 1930s, the Chinese population in Winnipeg shrunk. By 1939, only 19 Chinese laundries were still running, a staggering decline from the 150 laundries two decades earlier. Many Chinese men who lost their jobs turned to gambling as an escape. Some Chinese migrated out of Manitoba to other parts of Canada, while others returned to China. Tensions also ran high between different Chinese political groups, notably the city's Kuomintang supporters and the Communists.

The squabbling eased during World War II as the Chinese community focused on fundraising for the war effort against the Japanese. In 1939, despite the rampant unemployment caused by the Depression, Winnipeg's Chinese gathered $2000 in a single day for the Red Cross, enough money to help 2000 refugees. The city's Chinatown raised a total of $130,000 throughout the war.

Following the war, Chinese immigration to Canada resumed, but the city's Chinatown entered a period of decline. Younger generations had left Chinatown to find better jobs in other areas of the city and around the province. Throughout the 1960s and 1970s, newcomers mostly from Hong Kong settled outside of Chinatown in more middle-class areas such as Fort Richmond.

However, in 1979–80, Manitoba received 4000 refugees from Southeast Asia, including many ethnic Chinese. More than half of the refugees ended up in Winnipeg, which boosted the population in Chinatown. Several major development projects, including the building of a new seniors' housing complex and a shopping plaza, also helped to revitalize Chinatown. In 1987, another big development project, the Winnipeg Chinese Cultural and Community Centre, was a further boost to the Chinese community.

The Manitoba government, recognizing that immigration was one key to its future growth and success, opened an office in Hong Kong in 1985 to promote the province's economic opportunities. One year later, several Hong Kong business immigrants arrived in Manitoba and invested over $12 million in local businesses, creating more than 130 new jobs.

However, throughout the 1990s, many of Winnipeg's Chinese Canadian business owners struggled to maintain their profits because of the city's relatively low Chinese population. During the immigration surge leading up to the Hong Kong handover, the majority of new Chinese Canadians settled in Toronto and Vancouver.

By 2001, Winnipeg's Chinese population of about 11,000 ranked fourth largest among visible minorities in the city. There were more Filipinos, South Asians and African Canadians than Chinese. As of the early 21st century, Winnipeg's Chinatown is one of the smallest (and coldest) of Canada's major-city Chinatowns.

CHAPTER TEN

CHINATOWNS IN EASTERN CANADA

TORONTO

The Greater Toronto Area (GTA) is currently home to the most ethnic Chinese in the country (and has more Chinatowns than you can shake a stick at), but the Chinese community here got off to a slower start than its West Coast counterparts. It's believed that the first Chinese to arrive in Toronto came from the United States. The city's earliest Chinese-run laundries opened in the late 1870s, around the same time some Chinese had migrated from the U.S. to Montréal and Winnipeg, likely because of a massive recession. Word had spread about anti-Chinese attitudes in California and British Columbia, so a few Chinese ventured into Canada's more eastern regions. I hope they brought winter coats.

Toronto's first Chinatown was established close to the edge of Lake Ontario at the intersection of Dundas and Elizabeth streets. This neighbourhood was located near the first Union Station, built by the Grand Trunk Railway, which made it convenient for Chinese settlers arriving by rail.

By the 1890s, 24 Chinese laundries were operating in Toronto—a relatively small number compared to cities in other provinces, although it did represent around 43 percent of all laundry services in the city. By 1900, however, the number of laundries quadrupled, and somewhere between 150 and 200 Chinese were living in downtown Toronto. They also ran a restaurant, a couple of stores and several tea houses.

As with Canada's other Chinese communities, Toronto's Chinese-run businesses were often the targets of white hostility and discriminatory regulations. In 1918, for example, white business owners pushed for city hall to deny operating licences for Chinese laundries and restaurants. A year later, a mob of 400 white men ran through the streets of Chinatown, smashing windows and robbing stores. And as had happened in British Columbia, attempts were made to prevent Chinese cafe owners from hiring white waitresses.

The city's budding Chinatown was also a frequent punching-bag of the local press. A newspaper, which, interestingly, was called *Jack Canuck*, published an editorial that read:

> One need only stroll through the above mentioned block [King, Queen, Yonge and York Streets] and notice the throngs of Chinamen lounging in the streets and doorways to realize the "Yellow Peril" is more than a mere word in this city. The average citizen would stand aghast did he but realize the awful menace lurking behind the partitions or screens of some of these innocent appearing laundries and restaurants.

Christianity played a large role in Toronto's early Chinese community. One of the city's first Chinese Canadian organizations was the Chinese Christian Endeavour Society, a group that promoted famine relief and missionary work in China. By 1910, nearly half of Toronto's Chinese population, which numbered about 1000, was enrolled in classes at Christian churches. That year also saw the formation of the Chinese Christian Association (CCA). It provided English language classes and room and board for new Chinese immigrants and acted as a community leader in lieu of a more formal Chinese association such as the ones in the British Columbia. In later years, another Toronto-based Chinese Christian group, the Young Men's Christian Institute, organized Chinese communities from across Ontario to rally at Parliament against the Chinese Immigration Act.

Toronto's Chinese population remained relatively small in the early 20th century. By the time the federal government did shut down Chinese immigration in 1923, only about 2100 Chinese were living in Toronto. The population increased gradually after World War II, to 6700 by 1961, but most of the city's Chinese were soon forced to leave the first Chinatown.

Between the late 1950s and early 1960s, nearly two-thirds of the original Chinatown was destroyed to create space for Nathan Phillips Square and the new city hall. Many of the Chinese businesses and residences migrated west to the Dundas Street and Spadina Avenue area, forming a newer central Chinatown. Toward the late 1960s, new Chinese immigrants favoured settling in Ontario over British Columbia, which raised Toronto's Chinese population. Businesses grew in central Chinatown, while a few stores and services remained at the old location.

In 1967, city planners proposed wiping out the old Chinatown entirely, as it had fallen into disrepair, and many considered it to be an eyesore. Some councillors argued that keeping it would only encourage the existence of ethnic ghettos. But a movement started within the Chinese community to save the old Chinatown. Local businesswoman and community activist Jean B. Lumb led the Save Chinatown Committee, which gained support from other national Chinese groups and community leaders. Lumb (a fascinating person who we'll revisit later on) was successful in her campaign—city council agreed not to do away with the old Chinatown.

Lumb eventually became the first Chinese Canadian woman to be named to the Order of Canada, in part for her Chinatown preservation efforts. Old Chinatown remained, but by that time, the vast majority of new Chinese immigrants had settled in other parts of Toronto.

As the Chinese presence continued to grow in Toronto, a third Chinatown was born. This one is situated just east of the downtown core on Gerrard-Broadview Avenue. The relatively low rent and housing prices attracted new Chinese residents. The area is surrounded by gorgeous parks and is near the Don River. Chinatown East, as it came to be known, grew to overtake the first Chinatown but remains to this day much smaller than the Chinatown at Dundas and Spadina.

Meanwhile, the Dundas and Spadina Chinatown fought to preserve its residential nature in the 1970s. Developers wanted the city to zone the area for high-density residential and commercial uses, but many residents were concerned that the area would get too big and too busy. The debates got pretty heated, with newer Hong Kong immigrants choosing sides—some advocating for more commercial development, others wanting less urbanization. The city eventually enforced a compromise between the warring factions by allowing high-density development in some areas of Spadina and keeping Dundas Street low density. Neither side was very happy, apparently.

Throughout the 1980s and 1990s, the impending Hong Kong handover and the economic success of east Asian countries such as Taiwan and Singapore sparked a wave of immigration to the Toronto area that saw it overtake Vancouver as being home to the most Chinese in Canada.

The wealthier immigrants settled outside Toronto's central Chinatowns and in the suburban areas of Markham, Scarborough and Richmond Hill. Unlike most of the early Chinese immigrants, they had more financial means and probably better English skills. Although they wanted to stay connected with the Chinese community, these new immigrants also wanted to buy houses, to drive cars and to live like other middle-class suburban Canadians.

With so many Chinese living in Toronto's northern suburbs, Asian-themed malls began popping up to provide familiar stores, restaurants and entertainment for a fast-growing market. Initially, many new Chinese arrived in Scarborough, particularly in the Agincourt neighbourhood, which was the location of the first major Chinese mall, the Dragon Centre. Other malls soon followed.

As the Chinese Canadian population drifted north to the Markham–Scarborough border, the Pacific Mall and Market Village malls opened in the late 1990s. Combined, they feature over 500 stores and 1500 parking spaces. Advertised as the largest indoor Asian mall in North America, it has become one of the most popular places in the Toronto area to get bubble tea, see the latest clothing trends from Asia and party in a karaoke lounge, all in the same day. About a decade later, another large suburban mall, the Splendid China Tower, opened directly across from Pacific Mall. More Asian-themed malls are planned, which will turn this area into a major tourist destination for Chinese visitors as well as others looking for a slice of Chinese culture and entertainment.

There is also enough of a local market to sustain these malls. As of 2006, nearly two-thirds of Markham's population was foreign-born, with China (including Hong Kong) being the most common location of origin. Nearly half of Richmond Hill's residents are visible minorities, with ethnic Chinese making up more than 20 percent of those minorities.

The development of these new suburban Chinatowns provided strong economic boons to these areas but served to ignite tensions between the growing Chinese population and the broader community. During the mid-1990s influx of Chinese into Markham, non-Chinese residents and business owners often complained about increased traffic congestion and the lack of English signage in the Chinese commercial areas. Carole Bell, the city's deputy mayor at that time, believed the concentration of ethnic groups was leading to social conflict. She told the press that "everything's going Chinese," which sparked a wave of protest from the Chinese communities. But with the Chinese population now firmly entrenched in these areas, and Chinese investment driving further development, it appears that these monster theme malls are here to stay.

The Chinese in modern Toronto look to the city's Chinatowns for entertainment and fun rather than for protection from hostile neighbours. Chinese Canadians are better integrated than ever with mainstream society, and many non-Chinese Torontonians have become engaged and interested in Chinese culture. But Toronto's Chinatowns have an enduring legacy that shouldn't be forgotten. Much like the country's other major urban Chinese community, Vancouver, Toronto's Chinese population has accomplished a great deal toward raising the Chinese people's profile in Canada and challenging stereotypes and discrimination. The Chinese Canadian National Council, for example, was formed after a conference took place in Toronto addressing CTV's "Campus Giveaway" documentary. Asian gay and lesbian groups emerged in the 1980s, giving homosexual and trans-gendered Chinese Canadians a voice.

Other Toronto Chinese have earned high-profile positions within the community. Lawyer Susan Eng, endorsed by the province's then-premier Bob Rae, served for several years on the city's Police Services Board in the 1990s. Olivia Chow, a Hong Kong immigrant, was a popular city councillor for many years before being elected as a Member of Parliament for the Trinity-Spadina riding in 2006. She, and her husband Jack Layton, became two of the most recognizable members of the NDP during the late 20th century. There have been so many great stories about Chinese Canadians making a difference in Toronto, for all the city's residents, not just the Chinese. I'm positive more stories are destined to follow.

OTTAWA

The growth of Ottawa's Chinatown came largely after the 1960s, as immigration from Hong Kong increased dramatically. Before World War II, Ottawa's Chinatown population was a mere 300.

It's believed the first Chinese to come to our nation's capital was a man with the surname Tam in the late 1880s.

He was soon joined by others sharing this last name, although it was sometimes spelt "Hum" or "Hom."

Ottawa's early Chinese, like most other Chinese spreading across Canada, ran laundries or opened restaurants. Chinatown emerged on Albert Street, between Kent and O'Connor. As the city's civil service sector grew, so did the number of restaurants and laundries. By 1921, there were 16 Chinese-run restaurants in the city. As the decade progressed, the number of Chinese laundries peaked at 60. By 1943, about half of Ottawa's Chinese population worked in cafes and eateries, such as Boston Cafe and Capital Lunch. These places served Western-style food and actually employed a few white waitresses without too much of a hassle.

Ottawa's early Chinese community leaders took advantage of their unique position living in the country's capital by becoming politically engaged in international affairs. In 1915, teachers and students at Ottawa's Chinese school sent a telegram to the president of China appealing to him to declare war on Japan. In 1920, as droughts ravaged the northern countryside in mainland China, Ottawa's Chinese community formed the Association for Famine Relief. The group lobbied federal ministers to send revenue from the head tax to China and to send the starving people wheat shipments, but the request was refused. Other Chinese leaders and activists from across Canada often came to Ottawa to lobby the government on different causes, such as ending the head tax and, later, the Chinese immigration ban of 1923.

The Christian church was an important influence on Ottawa's Chinese community. Christian groups began teaching English to the city's Chinese residents as early as 1891. As the years passed, Christian Chinese Canadians formed many community organizations, including the Chinese Mission (later known as the Chinese United Church), the city's first Chinese congregation.

The Chinese Mission offered Chinese language classes and became the place where young Canadian-born Chinese came together for dances and fundraisers and to form sports teams. By 1931, almost 60 percent of Chinese people in Ottawa were Christians. Only Halifax, with 77 percent, had a higher ratio of Christian Chinese Canadians. It's suggested that, given the relatively small size of Ottawa's Chinese population, the Chinese residents joined church groups because bigger Chinese community associations, like the ones in Victoria and Vancouver, were largely absent from the nation's capital in the early 20th century.

Ottawa's Chinese population grew rapidly in the decades following World War II. Many of the city's Chinese residents obtained citizenship quickly after the immigration ban was lifted in 1947 and immediately sought to bring over their spouses and children. Many students from Hong Kong arrived in the 1950s to attend Ottawa's universities.

Throughout the late 1950s and 1960s, the city's Chinese community became divisive as fears of Communism penetrated into Canada. As the nation's capital, Ottawa often hosted foreign diplomats and trade missions, which sometimes sparked political tensions. In 1968, dozens of the city's Chinese residents wrote to Prime Minister Pierre Trudeau protesting Canada's official recognition of Communist China as a country. Some Chinese Canadian groups later expressed dismay when the Chinese government established an embassy in Ottawa. Other Chinese Canadians were more supportive of China. Ottawa's Chinese population grew significantly throughout the 1970s after immigration reforms made the selection process less restrictive.

The city's Chinese population increased from 3600 to 8200 during this decade, mostly driven by immigration from Hong Kong. In 1979, city officials and church groups joined together to sponsor 3800 refugees from Vietnam, many of whom were ethnic Chinese. Chinese businesses expanded as well, moving onto Somerset Street. The Hong Kong immigrants started many organizations in Ottawa, including the development of the National Capital Chinese Community Newsletter and the Ottawa Chinese Community Service Centre. They also started a local Chinese-language TV station.

In 1986, Chinese commercial groups proposed shaping the area into a more distinctive Chinatown to attract more customers and Chinese investment. By this time, the Somerset area had become very multicultural and featured many Southeast Asian stores as well. City officials and community groups joined the debate, and some argued against highlighting one particular culture. After several consultations, the plan to make Chinatown even more Chinese was dropped.

By the mid-1990s, the Chinese community's demographics shifted in favour of mainland Chinese, who began immigrating to Ottawa in larger numbers. The largest Chinese churches began offering their weekly services in Mandarin. While Hong Kong immigrants typically had backgrounds in finance and business, many of the city's new mainland Chinese had high education levels and were trained as doctors, engineers, scholars and information technology experts. The mainland Chinese started their own weekly newspaper, the *Canada China News,* and formed the Ottawa Mandarin Alliance Church. By the start of the 21st century,

Ottawa's Chinese community, which had only boasted a few hundred Chinese before 1945, became the sixth largest in Canada.

MONTRÉAL

The Chinese have a fascinating history in Montréal, having first arrived there long before the gold rush began in British Columbia. Montréal, Canada's second-oldest city, after Québec City, was first settled in 1535. A small number Chinese found work in the city as servants, with one Chinese confirmed as living in the Saint Joseph district as early as 1825. Forty years later, some Chinese attended Saint-Laurent School. In the early 1880s, somewhere between 7 and 30 Chinese lived in Montréal; most of them arrived via the United States as the CPR hadn't been completed yet.

The Chinese population grew quickly, blossoming to 900 members by 1901, making it the third-largest Chinese community in Canada. Most of Montréal's early Chinese belonged to three surname clans: the Lees, the Wongs and the Homs (also known as the Tams). Chinatown was situated near Dufferin Park, in an area once populated by Jewish Canadians.

Throughout the early 20th century, the Chinese opened over 1000 laundries, although only a quarter of them survived. Cafes and restaurants were also popular businesses for the Chinese, and, by 1921, there were more than 50 Chinese-run eateries.

As in the other Canadian Chinatowns, the Chinese immigrants brought with them some conflicts from the old country. In December 1933, the Chinese Freemasons and Kuomintang Nationalist Party members got into a serious ruckus on the streets of Chinatown. According to reports, about 45 people were seen wielding

Chinese swords, knives and clubs! After about 15 minutes of fighting, several men lay unconscious. Police arrested 25 people in connection with the Chinatown showdown. The Catholic Church became extremely influential in the Chinese community in Montréal. Nuns provided both England and French language classes, taught primary school to Chinese children and helped organize funding for the Montréal Chinese Hospital. Learning French was particularly useful (and a unique aspect of the Montréal Chinese) for the Chinese laundry and cafe owners who interacted with French-speaking Montréalers on a daily basis.

In World War II, 40 Montréal Chinese enlisted in the military, the majority of them being first-generation Canadians. Others in Chinatown helped raise funds and set up a local security brigade to protect the area. The group ran military drills, did firearms testing and offered first-aid training.

The Chinese population in Montréal shrank throughout the immigration ban years between 1923 and 1947 but shot up afterward. Chinatown's revitalization was brief, however, as the city's development cut into the neighbourhood during the 1960s and 1970s. Shops were bulldozed to widen streets, and the Chinese hospital was closed for health and safety reasons. The hospital reopened a few years later but away from Chinatown.

The Chinese United Church was torn down to make way for the Hydro Québec offices, and many residents were relocated. In 1972, the Québec government decided to build the Guy Favreau Complex, a massive building that included residential and office towers, in Montréal's Chinatown. Despite the protest from the city's Chinese community, construction went ahead, eating up 2.4 hectares of Chinatown. Many historic

Chinatown buildings were demolished, although the Chinese Catholic Church, a designated historic site, was spared.

Meanwhile, Montréal found itself in the middle of a wave of Québec nationalism. In 1970, the governing Québec Liberal Party introduced legislation to make French the official language of the province. A number of Anglophone and Chinese families left Montréal in the late 1970s. In 1980, the province held its first referendum vote to determine whether Québec should pursue sovereignty apart from Canada. Although nearly 60 percent of Québeckers voted *non* (or *bu shi,* in Mandarin), the political uncertainty led to a lull in business investment. The Chinese, however, soon helped to fill that gap.

Entering the mid-1980s, the Québec government actively recruited economic-class Chinese immigrants by setting up an office in Hong Kong and promoting the province's affordable electricity and low rental costs. Québec accepted almost 15,000 business immigrants from Hong Kong, Taiwan and mainland China. These new immigrants invested $871 million by establishing businesses and creating 9000 jobs. Newer Chinatowns grew in other parts of the city, including Saint Catherine Street near Concordia University and the suburb of Brossard.

Despite this flurry of economic activity, many Chinese immigrants who landed in Montréal didn't stay. They found learning French to be difficult and knew there was little job advancement for those who couldn't speak the language. Many ended up settling in Toronto or Vancouver instead, where they believed the job market was preferable. The French language issue also arose within the Chinese community after language inspectors in the late 1980s complained that Chinese stores didn't have enough French on their signs. Since 1985, the Québec government had passed laws requiring signs to be in French, as a way of protecting their official language in commercial activities.

The government demanded that Chinese business owners add French words to the signs and make them twice as prominent as the Chinese characters. Some within the Montréal community felt this was a bit heavy-handed: after all, it was the English presence they viewed as a threat, not the Chinese. Eventually, a compromise was reached—the signs were left alone if Chinese restaurant owners promised to feature more French on their menus.

Montréal's unique position as a gateway between English and French Canada places its Chinese community in a situation unlike any other in the country. The city's bilingual nature may have intimidated some Chinese immigrants (who often find learning one official language hard enough), which could explain why the Chinese are the fifth most populous visible minority group in Montréal. In Vancouver and Toronto, the two other largest cities in the country, the Chinese rank as the first and second largest visible minority group, respectively. As the 21st century continues, the Chinese population may continue to rise in Montréal: the city recently overtook Vancouver as the second most popular destination in Canada for new immigrants (Toronto is first).

HALIFAX

The first two Chinese people to settle in Halifax arrived in 1890. The pair set up a laundry on Duke Street and put the call out to their countrymen. More laundries popped up and the Chinese community began to grow.

By 1901, there were 106 Chinese in Nova Scotia. Much like the Chinese in many other Canadian communities, the early settlers in Halifax learned English through classes organized by the local churches. Christianity was an important influence in Halifax's Chinatown. In 1912, after several churches helped the Chinese community raise funds for a famine in China, about 50 Chinese students held a nice banquet for their Christian buddies. By 1930, nearly 80 percent of the Chinese in Halifax were Christians, the highest percent of any Canadian city. Ten years later, the proportion still remained high, at about 66 percent.

Not everyone was friendly to the Chinese, though. The soldiers and sailors stationed at the port and military facilities often gave the Chinese a hard time. In May 1918, a group of soldiers dragged a Chinese man out of his laundry onto the streets and beat him to a pulp because he asked for a ticket stub before returning their laundry. The next year, some drunk soldiers ate an expensive meal at a Chinese-run cafe and refused to pay the bill. When the Chinese owner complained, they knocked the tables over and started a fight. The police had to be called in.

In 1919, a riot broke out in Chinatown after hundreds of soldiers and locals ran amok in several Chinese restaurants, smashing chairs, tables, windows and looting the cash registers. Apparently, the Frisco Cafe was left unharmed only because the owner's white wife stood at the front door and cussed them out. Things got so out of control that the city police were powerless to stop the mayhem until backup from the military police arrived. It took years for the Chinese to get some compensation for the attack. Although no other mass incident occurred after this, fights still broke out occasionally in Chinatown.

The Chinese had been living in Halifax for nearly 30 years when the city's first Chinese Canadian baby was born, in June 1920. There weren't a lot of Chinese families in town. The following year, only two Chinese women were identified in the city's census. Interestingly enough, this gave Halifax the highest male-to-female ratio in Canada: 60 to one. Not all Chinese men were bachelors, though, as some partnered with Acadian women.

Halifax's importance as a military port helped to attract more Chinese people, as food services were in high demand throughout the World War II effort. Chinese-run cafes had proliferated between 1940 and the end of the war, and, by 1952, more than 40 such eateries had been established. Chinese cuisine became more popular, which led to an increase in restaurants and in the local Chinese population. Shortly after the repeal of the Chinese Immigration Act in 1947, a man named Freeman Hum landed in Halifax and began working as a waiter in various Chinese restaurants in the city. He later opened his own joint, employing more than 20 people. After his first successful venture, he founded the first Chinese drive-in and takeout restaurant.

Halifax is home to several universities and colleges, as well as research institutes. The city has attracted scholars from around the world, including China and Taiwan, and these Chinese students formed many community organizations and helped introduce Chinese culture to the masses. In 1970, for Chinese New Year, the Chinese Students Association presented the first lion dance in Halifax. Lion dances feature elaborate, colourful costumes, loud, percussive music and powerful, martial-arts-based movements—it must have been quite the sight for non-Chinese residents unfamiliar with the dance. Many of these students applied for landed immigrant status or Canadian citizenship, which boosted Halifax's Chinese population. By 1981, the number of Chinese in the city had risen to 1000. Two decades later, about 4000 Chinese resided in Halifax, about half of them students.

The Chinese population in Halifax is always in a state of flux, though. In the late 20th century, the economies of the Maritime provinces struggled with stagnation and the collapse of the fisheries, making jobs harder to come by. It's quite common for Halifax's Chinese graduates to move on to Toronto or Vancouver in search of employment opportunities, sometimes bringing their retirement-age parents with them.

As of the early 21st century, the Chinese in Halifax made up only about 10 percent of the city's visible minorities. African Canadians represent more than half of Halifax's visible minorities, followed by Canadians of Arab heritage. Some Chinese Canadians believe this historic cultural mix actually helped the Chinese integrate more smoothly with the broader society. Chuck Lee, a Chinese Canadian who grew up in Halifax in the early 20th century, credited the activism of the local African Canadian community for paving the way for the Chinese.

"Chinese Canadians have benefited by the black people's struggle against racism," Lee said. "The blacks acted as vanguards in the fight against bigotry and oppression. We Chinese were not so vocal, we mainly jumped on their bandwagon. We should be thankful to the blacks for their success and join them in the common struggle for equality and freedom."

Chinatowns represent a huge part of Chinese Canadian history because that's where most Chinese lived up until the latter half of the 20th century. Although all Canadian Chinatowns share similarities in their birth, evolution and, in many cases, decline, they also have unique legacies that will hopefully not be forgotten.

It's beautiful that today's Chinese Canadians are able to live and work among the broader Canadian community, no longer relegated to living in one or two city blocks. They've gained respect and recognition and are considered an important part of this country's social and cultural mosaic. But this type of inclusion only came after Chinatown leaders, activists and community members of the past fought hard for the rights of Chinese people and worked to change the unfair perceptions and stereotypes about the Chinese. It's a shame that many of these early Chinese Canadians never experienced the kind of compassion, acceptance and empathy for which Canadians have become known around the world.

In the past, Chinese Canadians were treated with contempt, seen as temporary visitors and then further criticized for sticking together in Chinatowns. As David Chuenyan Lai wrote in his excellent book *Chinatowns: Towns within Cities in Canada*, "The Chinese had always been accused of confining themselves to their Chinatown and refusing to be assimilated into the host society."

Won Alexander Cumyow, the first Canadian-born Chinese (in 1861 in Port Douglas, British Columbia), had this to say about the treatment of the Chinese in 1902:

> This unfriendliness and want of respect has caused a feeling of want of confidence among the Chinese, and it certainly has not tended to induce them to abandon their own ways and modes of life....My opinion is, that if

the Chinese were accorded the same respect as others here, they would prove themselves to be good citizens, and they would settle in the land with their wives and families.

Cumyow died in 1955, a few years after the Chinese immigration ban ended. I think he would have been proud to see how many Chinese and their families had settled in all parts of the country—and to see how many have proved themselves to be good citizens. The Chinese were eventually given the respect Cumyow talked about. But nothing was handed to them. They fought for every bit of it, especially in Chinatown.

Chapter Eleven

WOK 'N' ROLL

The famous American travelling chef and TV host Anthony Bourdain once wrote that inside every great cook "lurks the heart and soul of a Chinese guy....Chinese cooks and chefs are used to preparing food for customers who know what the f*** they're eating: what's good, where it's good, and when it's good. Next to them, we know nothing about food."

There are approximately 1.4 billion people on this planet who would absolutely concur with that statement. Any Chinese person will tell you that food is central to Chinese culture. From the sourcing and preparation of the ingredients, to the myriad cooking techniques, to the often elaborate presentation styles, food is very serious business. It's at the core of Chinese social life, as busy families, friends, neighbours and co-workers come together at meal times.

Most Chinese festivals and celebrations involve unique specialty dishes. Moon cakes, for example, are a rich pastry with lotus-seed filling consumed during the mid-autumn festival. At the annual *Duanwu Jie* (dragon boat festival), Chinese people eat rice dumplings made by stuffing glutinous rice and different sweet or savoury fillings in lotus leaves and then steaming them, kind of like a Chinese version of the Latin American corn tamale. Weddings are always followed by an elaborate Chinese banquet consisting of up to 10 dishes, including special soups and desserts that symbolize good luck and prosperity.

Food is such an important part of the social fabric that people in mainland China often greet each other by asking, "*Ni chi fan le ma?*" which means, "Have you eaten lunch/dinner, yet?" Try saying that to your Western friends next time in lieu of "Hello" and see what reaction you get. They'll probably expect you to invite them for a free meal. The Chinese, however, are merely interested in finding out what you've eaten and where you obtained it.

Having grown up in this food-crazy culture, I can tell you firsthand that, when asked what the world's best cuisine is, most Chinese people will subtly puff out their chests and firmly respond, "Chinese." This answer is often accompanied by a look of incredulity, as if to say, "Seriously? C'mon. What else is there?"

The level of pride Chinese people exhibit when discussing the culinary delights of their heritage never ceases to astound me. I vividly remember, as a child many years ago, attending a company Christmas party for my dad's work. For most of his life, he's been employed as a sales manager at an Ontario-based textiles manufacturer. It was a pretty good year for the company, so the affair was held in a swanky banquet hall west of Toronto that overlooked Lake Ontario.

Dinner was served buffet-style, and a magnificent spread of international delights, from salmon-studded sushi rolls to elaborate salads to crispy Indian samosas, anchored the dining room. I was eagerly ladling chilli-spiked chicken curry and fragrant basmati rice onto my plate when I overheard a conversation in Cantonese between a young Chinese businessman and his elderly father in line next to me.

Young businessman: "Hey, Dad, isn't this impressive? Look, they have this lovely rice."

Elderly man (sniffs): "But it's not even Chinese rice."

Yes, even plain white rice is a point of national pride for the Chinese.

Chinese food, in all its glorious regional varieties, is very much part of Canadian mainstream culinary culture these days. It's common now to see non-Chinese sitting in Chinatown restaurants, chowing down on exotic dishes such as preserved bean curd, marinated goose feet or sautéed geoduck clams (which, let's face it, bear more than a passing resemblance to a rather distinctive male body part). There's constant chatter on Canadian food blogs and website message boards about where to find the best Cantonese dim sum in the Prairies or what restaurant serves the tastiest shrimp won ton noodle soup in Québec. Hong Kong–style bakeries, offering rich, buttery egg-custard tarts, savoury spring rolls and dozens of varieties of sweet, stuffed buns, can now be found all across Canada's metropolitan cities, increasingly even in locations such as subway stations. These days, for some city folk, grabbing a cup of pearl milk tea and a Chinese coconut pastry is becoming as familiar as stopping off at Tim Hortons for a double-double and a honey cruller. The calories probably amount to the same, anyway.

Even McDonald's, a fast-food chain that's one of the most powerful and enduring symbols of mainstream Western culture, announced in 2009 that it would offer a "Spicy Szechwan" dipping sauce for its legendary chicken McNuggets. The sugary sauce may not be the most accurate representation of Szechwan region flavours, which is a bold, fiery style of cuisine that usually includes throat-burning amounts of garlic, red chillies and peppercorns. But hey, it's a step up in recognition from the more generic "Asian-inspired" "sweet and sour" or "plum" sauces. If McDonald's introduces Peking McDuck snackwraps, the Chinese in North America will know for sure they've made it.

As a Chinese Canadian, I find it absolutely wonderful to see non-Chinese Canadians embracing the full diversity of *authentic* Chinese cuisine. Most of this food wasn't introduced to Canada until the immigration reforms of the 1970s and the impending Hong Kong handover led to a surge of Chinese immigrants. These new Chinese Canadians had more financial capital than any other previous generation of immigrants, and many invested in Chinese restaurants. With a growing Chinese population in Canada to feed, these restaurants could profit by serving up traditional Chinese food.

While the general population is also now discovering the joys of Guangdong-style suckling pig or steaming hot, ginger-inflected pork dumplings made in the Shanghainese tradition, Chinese Canadian food—a distinctly North American spin on Chinese cuisine—remains the most popular incarnation among Canadians.

This is with good reason, because it's been eaten and enjoyed by Canadians almost as long as the Chinese have been here. In small towns all across the country, where populations are sometimes too small to even support a Kelsey's or Montana's franchise, you'll see a neighbour-hood restaurant run by a Chinese family, offering up sweet 'n' sour chicken balls, pork fried rice, stir-fried beef and broccoli as well as other dishes in the canon of classic Chinese Canadian cuisine. It's likely that the family-run restaurant has been there for years, and it's also likely that the single Chinese family represents most of, if not all, the entire Chinese population in that tiny town.

Chinese Canadian restaurants, especially the small-town variety, are an important part of Chinese Canadian history. They were started by Canada's first Chinese pio-neers, the ones who came here for the gold rush and the railway and who were forced to scatter across the coun-try after the work dried up, often in settlements near the rail line. The fascinating evolution of Chinese food in Canada begins with them.

THE BIRTH OF CHOP SUEY

The first Chinese cuisine made in Canada originated from the immigrants working in British Columbia's mining camp sites. With no refrigeration and little money to spend, Chinese labourers needed food that was cheap and didn't spoil easily. Meals were basic, working-man's fare—plain white rice boiled in metal trays, some preserved or dried meat, maybe a few soggy vegetables, all washed down by tea they brought with them from China.

In the late 1840s and early 1850s, when the Chinese first arrived to work in Canada, the Chinese workers got along relatively well with the area's Caucasian people. It was widely recognized that the Chinese were needed to fill in the drastic labour shortages. Naturally, in the collective spirit of slogging it, some of the miners shared their food and a few *gwai lo* (the Cantonese word for "ghost man" or Caucasian) received their first taste of Chinese-style cooking. One man, Walter Moberly, who was hired to work on a wagon road connecting the mines, wrote about dining with Chinese miners in 1859:

> The Chinamen received me kindly and made me some tea and mixed some flour and water and made thick cakes of dough which they cut into strips about an inch in width and boiled. They had no other provision but were looking forward to the spring run of salmon...

Chop suey, a concoction of stir-fried chopped meats (everything from bits of roasted pork to seafood such as shrimp and squid) and assorted vegetables, usually served over plain rice or fried noodles with a handful of bean sprouts, is one of the most iconic East-meets-West creations from this rough-and-tumble frontier period. It remains an important menu staple of nearly every Chinese Canadian restaurant, much beloved by busy working parents who can't figure out what to make for dinner and by post-secondary students looking for an affordable way to satisfy their hunger after a night of boisterous boozing.

The exact origin of this dish remains unclear and has been a source of lively debate among food scholars and chop suey connoisseurs. As with other things many Canadians enjoy, such as rock 'n' roll or Barack Obama, chop suey may actually be American by birth. According to one popular folk story, a Chinese chef in San Francisco created the dish during the gold rush era. As legend has it, some petulant customers had thrown the chef into a Gordon Ramsay–level of rage, and revenge was on his mind. The angry cook decided to throw together a rather unique off-menu special by frying up the day's discarded meat bits with some old vegetables and a little leftover broth. The unknowing patrons scarfed down the meal and, to the surprise and amusement of the chef, loved every bite. Some people say the actual name of chop suey stems from the Chinese cook's inability to accurately pronounce "chopped sewage" in English, but that seems a little far-fetched.

Another well-known story suggests chop suey was invented by a Chinese chef in New York City during the late 19th century after he was tasked with cooking a meal for a Chinese official visiting the U.S. Budgetary constraints forced this chef to get a little creative with his leftovers, resulting in the one-pot wonder. Another version of this story claims the Chinese chef desperately wanted to make some authentic homeland cuisine for the distinguished official but couldn't track down any of the proper ingredients and was forced to use Western products. This may explain why some early versions of chop suey included the use of iconic Western condiments such as Heinz tomato ketchup and Worcestershire sauce.

The veracity of all these accounts is highly questionable, and most food historians agree that chop suey was simply a humble stir-fry of odds and ends cooked up by Chinese miners and railway workers in Gold Mountain. It has been pointed out that peasants and farmers in Guangdong often cobbled together a dinner of *tsap seui* ("mixed food or leftovers"). Given that the majority of Chinese labourers in Canada were originally from this southern Chinese province, it's likely they ate a variation of *tsap seui* made up of whatever food scraps they could find in the work camps.

OTHER CHINESE DELIGHTS

Another popular westernized Chinese dish is chow mein, which, in my humble opinion, stands alongside chop suey and sweet 'n' sour chicken balls as Chinese Canadian cuisine's holy triumvirate of dishes. Chow mein is simply a mess of noodles (of which there are numerous varieties) stir-fried with bits of vegetables and usually meat or seafood or both. The sauce generally consists of the usual suspects: any combination of soy sauce, chilli peppers, garlic, oyster sauce and sesame oil, and sometimes a splash of rice wine or cooking sherry.

The origins of chow mein are far less murky than that of chop suey. There's no humorous mythology behind it, as most food scholars and anthropologists agree that *chow mein* (which literally means "stir-fried noodles") is based on similar noodle dishes eaten in China, especially in the northern regions. It's important to note that people in many Chinese regions have a tradition of cultivating wheat and using the flour to make noodles, dumpling wrappers and cake-like foods. Items such as eggs, cereal and different starches are added to the wheat flour, which, along with different methods of cutting and pulling the dough, accounts for the tremendous variation of wheat noodles in China. In northern parts of China, rice wasn't traditionally a key part of the diet, but wheat noodles (*mein* in Cantonese, *mian* in Mandarin) were.

Since the majority of Chinese immigrants in Canada came from Guangdong, which is a rice-producing region, it was largely assumed in North America that all Chinese people ate rice with every meal. The southern Chinese provinces are also famous for making noodles, but theirs are generally made from rice flour, which results in a flat white noodle called *fun* (Cantonese) or *fen* (Mandarin). Rice noodles have a much lighter texture than *mein*, are chewier and don't crisp up nearly as well during frying as wheat noodles do. *Fun* noodles are ubiquitous in Cantonese restaurants and are often wok-fried with beef and Chinese broccoli or served in a steaming bowl of broth with various barbecued meats.

But the wheat noodles, stir-fried until crunchy or steamed until soft, are what North American–style chow mein is best known for. Because Canada was historically a wheat-farming nation, it's likely that *mein* became the noodle of choice for Chinese cooks, despite most Chinese immigrants in Canada being from southern China. Labourers in Gold Mountain likely cooked up rudimentary noodle stir-fries with whatever they could get hold of. I'm sure for many Chinese living in the camps and in Chinatowns, chow mein was a relatively obtainable taste of home.

For the most part, the ingredients in the chow meins of the world aren't all that different, with the notable exception of the versions that use deep-fried "chow mein" noodles. You've probably seen them in your local grocery store, available in bags or tins, in the ethnic foods aisles. These ultra-crispy noodles are fried in batches until golden and then mixed in with the stir-fried meat and vegetables, usually with a handful of bean sprouts. They have a texture and crunch more akin to potato chips than noodles, and many Chinese Canadian restaurants still use them not only in chow mein dishes but also as a garnish for soups. No one's exactly sure how this kind of noodle came into existence, but most native Chinese people don't recognize it. It was definitely created in the West, probably to appeal to non-Chinese palates.

CHINESE FOOD IN EARLY CANADA (AND PRE-CONFEDERATION)

Throughout the frontier years, the only other places beyond the work camps to experience some real Chinese food were in British Columbia's Chinatowns, such as those in Barkerville, Yale and Victoria. When the gold rush died down and mining work slowed, Chinese labourers were often forced from the few remaining profitable sites. Some began running small restaurants and cafes or worked as cooks for wealthy families or on transport ships.

For the most part, Chinese-run eateries served either Caucasians or a Chinese clientele, but they almost never offered Chinese food exclusively. The majority of the cafes, especially the ones operating outside of China-town, deeper in the rural regions, offered food more in tune with Western palates—roast beef and chicken sandwiches, British-style meat pies, fruit pies, ice cream, food they never had in China. Just as with laundries, Chinese cafes charged less for food than most Western restaurants and became popular places for cheap eats and fast service. To reduce overhead, the owners usually lived above the restaurant and hired family members and friends who weren't opposed to accepting low wages.

By the late 19th century, in BC's Chinatowns you could find a couple of chop suey houses and a few small places that specialized in comfort foods from Guangdong prov-ince that only Chinese people ate. There was also food on the streets—in vegetable and fruit market stalls as well as offerings of Chinese-style candied fruits, spices, herbs,

Chinese-run cafés in the early 20th century, like this one in Lacombe, Alberta, were popular for serving up reasonably priced Western-style food.

teas and other imported items from China. Eventually, as BC's Chinese population increased, restaurants appeared that could cater a traditional Chinese banquet (which usually feature up to 10 carefully prepared meat and seafood courses) for the area's small number of wealthy Chinese merchant families. These elaborate feasts take place on special occasions, such as Chinese New Year, weddings or visits by distinguished guests. It was a big deal to be invited to a Chinese banquet. A woman named Grace Lee, born in Victoria in 1902, recalled one such event:

> When I was a child, there was this very rich Chinese man who invited only the Chinese to dinner in his garden at his home once a year. Those were very happy occasions. In those days, there were a few very rich Chinese here.

The rich women were very grand. Whenever they were invited out for dinner, they would wrap their beautiful clothes in a bundle and change when they got to their destination. Then they would change back into their street clothes when they left. It was very grand! Even the children had to change clothes.

To the non-Chinese, however, Chinatown was seen as a filthy, disease-ridden place and the last place you'd want to have a meal. Unfortunately, there was a kernel of truth to this: many Chinese immigrants were forced to live in terrible conditions, huddled together in boarding houses, and they lacked access to the same quality of medical services as white Canadians.

Most *gwai lo* believed Chinese food was about as appetizing as eating a casserole made of torn leather boots and shredded newspaper. In his book *China to Chinatown: Chinese Food in the West*, author J.A.G. Roberts wrote that, as anti-Chinese sentiment spread, one of the earliest and most common complaints was about "the cheapness of the diet on which Chinese labourers subsisted."

In 1859, the *British Colonist* newspaper, based in Victoria, carried an article that remarked:

> It may do very well for the people in the cities, the merchants, the ship owners and steam boat men to talk in favour of the Chinese, but when a white man is placed alongside a company of these creatures, imported from abroad, and fed on rice and dog-fish, and made to measure the price of his day's work by the price of theirs, there will be complaining and dissatisfaction.

The racism against the Chinese in the early years led to the circulation of many rumours and negative stereotypes about Chinese food. You know, that the Chinese eat dogs and cats, and that Chinese restaurant owners are so cheap they'll use Fido or Garfield as a chicken substitute in your chow mein—that kind of stuff.

Indeed, it was socially acceptable in China to eat dog meat for centuries, but it wasn't particularly widespread. This practice occurred mostly in remote rural areas, and the dogs that were cooked were specifically bred for that purpose. So it wasn't as if people were taking someone's pet and dumping it into a stew pot. People ate cats too, but usually only in times of severe famine when almost nothing else was available.

Making meals out of dogs and cats was also not limited to Asian cultures. Both of these animals were consumed in Germany during times of crisis or war. Frederick the Great referred to dog meat as "blockade mutton" (somehow, "dog meat" still sounds more appetizing). In fact, the sale of dog meat in Germany wasn't officially prohibited until 1986. It's also been reported that rural parts of Switzerland have a tradition of eating cured dog sausages and dog jerky. Historical documents also indicate that people in France lined up outside butchers' shops for dog and cat meat in the late 19th century.

At any rate, this practice was left behind by immigrants of any ethnicity when they came to Canada. Yet Chinese people and their cuisine were still singled out as being savage and shamelessly cheap. Some historians believe that rumours of pet and rodent cooking were often spread by competitors angry at the Chinese for attracting their customers by offering more affordable prices.

The strong racial tension during the early 20th century made it difficult for Chinese restaurants to attract non-Chinese customers, but some joints did prosper and even employed a few white waitresses. Restaurant owners in smaller towns, especially in the Prairies, gained some measure of respect and even felt part of the community.

In British Columbia, however, the province with the largest Chinese population in Canada until the middle of the 20th century, Chinatown restaurants were largely banned from hiring white employees. This law was not rigorously enforced, but it reflected the popular social attitudes of the time: Chinese men should be limited in their contact with white women.

In 1931, after a white waitress was found murdered, allegedly by her Chinese lover, the issue attracted scathing attention and led to a lengthy showdown between Chinese proprietors and city officials in Vancouver over the rights of Chinese restaurants. It was declared that Chinese-run restaurants in the city could only employ white waitresses if they served Western food to Caucasian customers. This must have been a bitter pill to swallow, however, because during the Great Depression of the 1930s, Chinese-run cafes weren't allowed to accept welfare meal coupons.

The attitudes toward the Chinese, and Chinese cuisine by extension, began to change after World War II began. China and Canada were allies, and although Chinese Canadians were still generally treated as second-class citizens (actually, the vast majority didn't have Canadian citizenship), the Caucasians and Chinese shared common enemies. The image of the Chinese improved dramatically, as did the reputation of Chinese cuisine. Chinatown went from being an undesirable part of town to a popular tourist attraction for non-Chinese to hunt for bargains and to sample delicious, exotic foods.

It was soon common to spot several *gwai lo* sitting in the neighbourhood's chop suey houses.

Made in Chinese Canada

Canada's culinary history, compared to those of many other countries around the world, is relatively young, and the cuisine generally reflects the wide diversity of our land and people. There are a few distinctly Canadian culinary traditions—poutine, the artery-clogging but absolutely addictive combination of crisp French fries, cheese curds (not shredded!) and dark gravy, springs to mind immediately. You could add Montréal smoked meat and beaver tails to that short list. Many of these foods derive their influence from our English, French and Eastern European settlers.

Although Canadians definitely enjoy their Chinese food, it's still considered essentially Chinese and not particularly Canadian, the perception being that dishes like *cha siu* (sweet barbecued pork—a favourite of action star Jackie Chan) or won tons were invented outside of Canada.

But there is one Chinese-influenced dish that has become a proud, distinctly Canadian gastronomic tradition. Even more specifically, it's a proud Albertan gastronomic tradition. Ginger beef—tender strips of beef that are battered and fried until crispy, then smothered in a sweet-and-spicy ginger-infused sauce—was born in Canada to proud Chinese Canadians in 1975. Ginger beef has been widely consumed and adopted by the majority of other Chinese Canadian restaurants in the province ever since.

Although a few stories about the origin of this local food legend are in circulation, by most accounts, the man who created ginger beef in Canada is named George

Wong, a trained chef from Beijing who immigrated to Calgary. George, his wife, Lily, and their daughters worked in a family-run restaurant called the Silver Inn in Calgary. The menu was pretty eclectic initially; they served burgers and French fries alongside more traditional northern Chinese items such as pork dumplings and cashew chicken. Of course, the familiar hamburger outsold the exotic dumpling in the beginning, but, eventually, locals began gravitating more toward the Chinese food.

In his ambition to craft more Chinese dishes that would appeal to Western tastes, Wong re-jigged a customary Chinese beef dish. Traditional Chinese cuisine often features strips of beef as a main ingredient, but it's usually marinated and then stir-fried quickly in a searing hot pan. Drawing on his previous experiences of working as a cook in England, Wong knew that English pub food (battered and fried fish, French fries, fried meat pies—pretty much anything that can fit into a deep fryer) was also popular in Canada. Crispy fried foods tended to hold up better in take-out containers and were the preferred snacks of choice during long periods of beer drinking.

The new beef dish was an immediate hit. It was originally named "deep fried shredded beef in chilli sauce," but customers kept asking for the gingery-tasting beef. Thus, ginger beef was born.

Something else that has been synonymous with Chinese Canadian food is buffet restaurants. While most authentic Chinese restaurants serve up their meals a la carte, most Chinese Canadian restaurants seem to fall into one of two categories: they're either cozy take-out joints or all-you-can-eat food fests. Chinese Canadian buffets vary in size and scope as well. Many family-run places in small towns may feature a dozen or so offerings spread over one or two steam tables, while mammoth franchises, such as Ontario's Mandarin chain, serve up to 200 items and include sushi bars and grill stations offering freshly barbecued food.

It's not clear when or where the first Chinese-run buffet restaurant appeared, although some people believe the trend originated in Gastown (part of Vancouver, British Columbia), as an easy way to feed loggers and mill workers. Buffets have become very popular in Canada, and the formula for success echoes the Chinese-run cafes of the early 20th century: serve a wide array of food to appeal to a broad spectrum of tastes and charge reasonable prices.

At a Chinese Canadian buffet restaurant, trays of vegetable fried rice sit next to a vat of cherry red sweet-and-sour sauce. For the best example of cross-cultural culinary interaction, head straight for the dessert bar. You'll likely spot a plate of Nanaimo bars—those buttery, sugary, chocolate-topped treats—lounging next to Chinese almond cookies and coconut jelly squares.

It's a strategy that has worked for the Chinese in Canada for decades. Chinese Canadian restaurants today seem to continue to draw inspiration from early 20th-century diners and lounges. Sit down at a table and you'll probably see a paper placemat explaining the Chinese zodiac. Or you'll see an illustrated cocktail menu that was probably printed in the 1970s, when drinks such as Brandy Alexanders and Pink Cadillacs were still fashionable. Even the ultra-modern Mandarin restaurants still serve cocktails with umbrella hats and fruit skewers.

Other popular food trends in Canada originated outside the country but have worked their way into our culture.

One of the most fascinating culinary phenomena in North America has been the introduction of bubble tea. Bubble tea, also known as pearl milk tea, is a kind of chilled tea drink that's mixed with fruit juices, milk, ice-cream or flavoured syrups such as chocolate or almond. You can often find them infused with exotic flavours such as nutty taro root, lychee or jackfruit. The "bubbles" come from the addition of small, chewy, slightly sweet tapioca balls that often require a wider-than-usual plastic straw to get at them. The result is an odd but refreshing and delicious beverage you can both sip and eat.

Bubble tea first emerged in Taiwan in the early 1980s. Taiwan, like other major Asian cities, is well known for having vibrant night markets—crowded places filled with hawker stands where people can hang out and buy cheap clothes, electronics, snacks and drinks. It's kind of a like a fairground, only with fewer animals and rides and more pirated DVDs. According to the Bubble Tea Canada website, some ingenious Taiwanese vendor, whose name is now lost to history, invented the first incarnation of the drink by shaking his chilled tea to create a pleasant bubble effect. The idea caught on, and before long, other drinks vendors came up with the idea to mix in tapioca pearls for double the bubbles.

Just like film director Ang Lee, another Taiwanese export, bubble tea gained critical acclaim all over Asia before catching the attention of people in North America. Bubble tea cafes began appearing in the continent's Chinatowns and Chinese malls, and, pretty soon, articles about this exotic and fun new drink appeared in major metropolitan newspapers.

Bubble tea, like other Asian youth trends before it (for example, the Dance Dance Revolution video game), has succeeded splendidly in North America because of the high concentration of ethnic Asian populations. Bubble tea franchises have become a popular business opportunity, and it's common to see tea kiosks operating out of suburban Canadian malls and retail parks. Many upscale pan-Asian restaurants also include bubble tea cocktails on their drinks menu.

Some observers noted (with some amusement) that while bubble tea succeeded, another beverage with chewy, colourful bubbles, called Orbitz, failed miserably when it was introduced around 1997. The fruit-flavoured bottled drink was a Canadian product, manufactured by the Vancouver-based Clearly Canadian Beverage Corporation. People familiar with this short-lived drink will recall it bore a vague resemblance to a lava lamp. Perhaps it tasted similar as well.

Another interesting trend is the places where people are getting their Chinese food and ingredients. For the longest time, authentic Chinese products and sauces could only be found at Chinese grocery stores in Chinatown. But Chinese supermarkets are increasingly entering the suburbs, where many new Chinese immigrants are settling.

A remarkable Chinese Canadian supermarket success story emerged in the 1990s. Cindy Lee was a housewife living in Vancouver with her husband and three young children. One rainy day, Cindy took her kids shopping. Her youngest son had to use the toilet, so she herded her children from store to store trying to find a washroom. They didn't find one in time, and her son ended up wetting himself. Frustrated, Cindy wondered why more stores in Canada didn't provide a simple thing like a washroom for their customers.

Cindy and her husband, Jack, a local real estate developer and food importer, decided to start their own store (with access to washrooms). Their concept was to offer a one-stop grocery-shopping experience for Chinese (and other Asian) and non-Chinese customers. They'd sell Chef Boyardee and Tropicana orange juice along with packages of rice noodles and jars of Malaysian curry sauces.

Although Asian grocery stores have existed in Canada for years, they tended to be small, crowded and probably intimidating to many Caucasians. The Lees' store would feature huge aisles and ample parking, like the Loblaws, Safeway or Metro big-chain supermarkets. They named it T&T. The "T"s come from the initials of Lee's first investors, Tawa Supermarket Inc. and Tung Yee (Taiwan-based Uni-President Enterprises Corp.). The Lees opened the first store in 1993.

A T&T supermarket is more like a food playground than a grocery store and usually contains a food court where people can purchase hot, authentic Chinese food. Some stores offer fresh dim sum, Chinese barbecue and other Asian delights such as sushi and bubble tea. During festivals and around Chinese New Year, the stores are typically adorned with decorations, and specialty foods are usually on sale.

Since the original store opened, T&T has become Canada's largest Asian-themed national supermarket chain. As of 2009, the company boasted 18 stores across the country, including eight locations in the greater Vancouver area, four in Alberta and six in Ontario. In 2009, Loblaws, one of Canada's biggest supermarket chains, purchased the T&T empire for about $225 million.

CANADA'S WOK 'N' ROLL STAR

If you lived in Canada during the 1980s and '90s and had a television, then you've likely caught an episode or two of an afternoon cooking show called *Wok with Yan*. It was originally produced by CBC television and starred a charismatic, highly excitable Hong Kong–born chef named Stephen Yan.

These days, cooking shows have reached new levels of popularity, and the chefs who host the shows have become celebrities. There are shows that focus on a vast range of ethnic cuisine with a diverse range of hosts to match—from *David Rocco's Dolce Vita* to *French Food at Home with Laura Calder*.

But in Canada 30 years ago, choices for cooking shows were slim pickings indeed. You pretty much had Julia Child and *The Urban Peasant* with James Barber (an excellent program and an iconic slice of Canadiana). Chinese cuisine was still an exotic delight considered by most non-Chinese as available only from restaurants.

Stephen Yan, who had two restaurants in the Vancouver area, burst onto the culinary TV scene and demystified Chinese cooking to mainstream Canadian audiences. He had cooking chops, certainly, but it was his enthusiastic personality and oddball humour that won him adoring fans. Before Emeril Lagasse rocketed to celebrity chef status with his "BAM!" and "Kick it up a notch!" catchphrases and live studio audiences, Yan combined television cooking with showmanship, in his own unique, Chinese-inflected style.

He's probably best remembered for donning a new apron every episode that had some cheesy, yet charming pun involving woks scribbled on it. Some of my own personal favourites include "Wok Goes in Must Come Out,"

"Danger, Men at Wok," "Wok This Way," "Keep on Wokking in the Free World," "Wok's New, Pussycat?" and the clever nod to hockey's place in Canadian culture, "Wokkey Night In Canada."

Yan had a thick Cantonese accent and often used Chinese-inspired pidgin English expressions such as "Long time, no see!" But he was a widely admired television personality, and I'm betting part of the reason he became so successful was that he didn't try to hide his ethnicity in order to gain acceptance among mainstream Canadian audiences. He was kooky and funny and foreign, but authentic.

For many non-Chinese in the 1980s, *Wok with Yan* was their first real exposure to traditional Chinese cooking. Yan went beyond egg rolls and chicken balls and often featured some of the perhaps more intimidating ingredients of classic Chinese cuisine, such as squid and prawns with the heads intact. He often brought up audience members to help him prep the food and would gently tease them if they seemed squeamish. His unbridled affection and enthusiasm for Chinese culture and cooking was infectious, and he became an unlikely Chinese Canadian media star. And I'm sure for many ethnic Chinese like myself, it was refreshing to see a Chinese man with a thick accent gain such mainstream popularity without having to be a kung-fu master.

Yan went on to achieve a certain level of fame outside Canada as well. He appeared on the biggest American talk shows, including *Late Night with David Letterman, Good Morning America,* and *Live with Regis and Kelly.* He also won audiences in Asia and Australia. Yan followed up the *Wok with Yan* series with several cookbooks and a travel show called *Wok's Up?*

The man responsible for bringing real Chinese food to Canadian TV has largely disappeared from the spotlight since the late 1990s. It's not really clear what he's up to these days. But thanks in part to his legendary cooking show and his ardent passion for Chinese cuisine, people of every ethnicity are more knowledgeable about Chinese food and are more open than ever to exploring it, both in restaurants and through making it at home. Stephen Yan may no longer be on TV, but he was instrumental in helping Chinese cuisine take a star turn in Canada, and it continues to win new fans every day.

Chapter Twelve

HEALTH AND MEDICINE

Besides Chinese cuisine, the next biggest aspect of Chinese culture that has gained mainstream acceptance in Canada in recent years is health and medicine. Like people from many other countries, Canadians are increasingly becoming concerned with healthy living and extending their lives as long—and as comfortably—as possible. We're all watching what we eat and worrying about where our food comes from. We're even cramming vitamins into our bottled water. You can hardly turn on your television or flip through a magazine without seeing advertisements for newfangled detoxing/weight-losing/purifying/antioxidant-rich/colon-cleansing/brain-boosting/organic health products.

In an effort to cover all the bases, many Canadians are now looking beyond traditional Western medicine and health practices to Chinese ones. And why not? The Chinese civilization has been around for over 5000 years.

They've probably picked up a few health tricks over time to keep their population going. According to a National Population and Health Survey conducted by Statistics Canada in 1998–99, nearly four million people aged 18 and over consulted an alternative (which includes traditional Chinese medicine) health care provider over the 12-month period.

Health (both physical and mental) is extremely important in Chinese culture, which is why one of the most common types of stores you'll see in Chinatown or in Chinese-themed malls are herbal remedy stores. These places are stocked wall-to-wall with tubs of dried fruits, roots, visually unidentifiable plants and even more bizarre items such as preserved deer antlers (good for relieving arthritis, apparently) and dried earthworm powder (just the thing for thrombosis). The Chinese believe there is a drink or food to treat almost any malady. And just like Buckley's cough medicine, it usually tastes awful, but they think it works. And so do a growing number of Canadians.

This chapter explores some of the more popular forms of Chinese health and medicine that Canadians have embraced over the years. Some of these traditional Chinese practices now seem as normal to mainstream Canadians as universal health care and Vicks VapoRub. But before I go into that, it would be prudent to look at some of the basic philosophy behind the Chinese approach to healthy living. You could spend years studying the ins and outs of this fascinating and complex medical system, but I'll just touch on the main concepts.

YIN AND YANG
The underlying philosophy behind traditional Chinese medicine revolves around the concept of yin and yang.

Yin and yang are opposite forces: they could represent cold and hot, north and south, tranquil and aggressive, feminine and masculine, and so on. These forces are perpetually at odds with one another but also complement each other—kind of like Britney Spears and the paparazzi —because they both need each other to survive.

Fully understanding the concept of yin and yang can be challenging, but most people would tend to agree that living in extremes will wear down your body pretty quickly. Sleeping less than seven hours each night can weaken your immune system and lead to weight gain and hypertension. But on the other hand, scientists have recently suggested that sleeping significantly more than seven hours may lead to an increased risk of diabetes, depression and cancer. Getting our daily required amount of vitamins is essential to healthy living, but gulping down too many vitamin supplements (which some people consume like Skittles candy these days) can trigger toxic reactions in your body. Balance is the key.

The Chinese believe the human body is a sophisticated collection of interconnected parts, and that an imbalance between your body's yins and yangs can cause illness or infection. The body's organs and functions are classified under *wu xing*, or what are known as the five elements: wood, fire, earth, metal and water. In traditional Chinese medicine, these elements are used to interpret the connection between the human body and the environment. It's a very holistic approach. Western medicine—the proponents of Chinese or Eastern medicine often argue—tends to treat specific symptoms and diseases instead.

The body's parts and functions are all unified by the body's *qi* (sometimes pronounced "chi"), which can be described as an energy flow. In Chinese medicine, *qi* is the vital energy force that controls the workings of the body and the mind. This energy travels through a network of pathways called meridians, each of which correspond to different organ functions. When your *qi* flow is out of whack, so are your five elements as well as your yins and yangs. Much of traditional Chinese healing focuses on restoring or strengthening *qi* flow through tai chi and *qigong* (physical manipulation), acupuncture (pressure points) or herbal teas (medicines).

TAI CHI

One of the most popular physical activities related to Chinese medicine is the martial art *tai chi chuan*. Literally translated, it means something like "supreme ultimate fist," which sounds mystical and powerful. I find it unfortunate that most Western forms of exercise lack names that are similarly butt-kicking yet poetic. Imagine if power walking was referred to as "transcendent feet gliding." Or if water aerobics were called something like "celestial dragon splashing." I'd sign up in a second.

In actuality, tai chi isn't a hard-hitting style of fighting that "supreme ultimate fist" would suggest. It's based on traditional Chinese martial arts, but the movements are performed much more gently and much slower. The focus in tai chi is not to generate knock-out power but to control your breathing and energy. As with other forms of traditional Chinese medicine, tai chi's principles are rooted in yin and yang. Performing the body movements with balance and proper posture are key. Doing so will help cultivate your *qi* energy, practitioners say.

No one is exactly sure where tai chi originated. Some scholars point out that lines from the *Tao Te Ching*, the classic Chinese text (thought to be written around the third-century B.C.E.) refers to the concept of tai chi:

"Yield and overcome; bend and be straight; empty and be full." The first systematized version of tai chi is said to have emerged in the 1600s.

There are five traditional styles of tai chi, each named after the family who developed it. The Chen style is named after the Chen clan of Chenjiagou village in Henan province. The Chen style is characterized by lower stances, bursts of power and even weapons training. The four other forms, of which we'll discuss just one, evolved from the Chen style, each developing their own unique qualities. The Yang style, created in the 18th century, probably has the most practitioners. It's a less aggressive form of tai chi, likely the style you've seen elderly Chinese gracefully practise in public parks.

There are two main types of tai chi training. The solo form is a sequence of movements—done as a routine—performed by an individual. The length of the movement patterns varies, but tai chi, despite its gentle appearance, can get quite demanding, both physically and mentally, and the longest routine involves no fewer than 108 moves.

The other most common kind of tai chi practice is called "pushing hands," which is a routine performed with a partner. Pushing hands resembles slow-motion hand-to-hand combat, with the participants using their hands to jostle for position. It's meant to be an exercise in controlling each other's energy and sharpening the reflexes and concentration.

Tai chi has grown immensely in Canada, especially with non-Chinese. The purported health benefits are what attract people most. Both the Canadian Pain Coalition and the Public Health Agency of Canada recommend tai chi as an exercise for people with chronic pain or low energy. Tai chi's low-impact movements and go-at-your-own pace have made it a popular activity among Canadians with chronic fatigue syndrome, multiple sclerosis and fibromyalgia. Studies have shown that doing tai chi can help relieve pain from osteoarthritis, which affects nearly one in ten Canadians, according to the Arthritis Society in 2009.

People are interested in tai chi for the mental and spiritual workout as well. A home-grown Canadian version of tai chi incorporates Taoist and Buddhist study. Taoist monk Master Moy Lin-shin immigrated to Toronto and in 1970 founded the Taoist Tai Chi Society. His brand of tai chi quickly spread across the country and the world. As of 2009, there were more than 40,000 members of the society worldwide, including 15,000 in Canada.

In 2007, members and friends of the society opened a new $20-million temple at the International Taoist Tai Chi Society's property in Orangeville, Ontario. The beautiful Fung Loy Kok Temple was paid for by donations and is at the heart of a big complex known as the Quiet Cultivation Centre. This training centre includes residences for people studying tai chi and a health building with 72 beds for people with chronic illnesses. The grand opening of the Fung Loy Kok Temple was preceded in the morning by a mass tai chi demonstration at Nathan Phillips Square in downtown Toronto and a parade of 2000 tai chi enthusiasts down Yonge Street. The excitement of the event was as if the Maple Leafs had won a playoff series, except more polite.

QIGONG

Qigong, which can be loosely translated as "life force or energy work," is a meditative martial art that's often associated with tai chi but isn't as commonly practised in North America. Whereas tai chi involves many body movements, *qigong* is a series of breathing and concentration techniques that could essentially be done by barely moving at all.

As with tai chi, *qigong*'s origins are unclear. Some believe that monks studying kung fu practised deep breathing to aid them in their training. Others say that *qigong* was developed in the 1950s by the Chinese government as a way to preserve traditional Chinese health philosophy and to offer an alternative to Western medicine.

The health claims of *qigong* are similar to those of tai chi: followers say running through the exercises helps to reduce stress, improve circulation and lessen pain. Others, the hardest-of-the-hardcore *qigong* types, believe that cultivating *qi* (chi) can lead to enormous, almost superhuman power and incredible resistance to physical pain or illness. You may have seen these people on television: typically, they do a few stretches, take a few deep breaths and then lie on a bed of nails with a block of ice on their stomachs as someone else strikes the ice with a giant hammer. You can watch similar videos on the website YouTube.

Although it's generally accepted that *qigong*'s deep breathing and concentration exercises yield some health benefits, the more extreme claims (such as projecting *qi* externally to heal someone's disease) made by some *qigong* practitioners have been met with scepticism by the scientific community. Not a lot of substantial academic research has been conducted on the subject. But *qigong*, in all its various forms, has become hugely popular in China and is gaining more momentum in the West as well.

Interestingly enough, *qigong*'s popularity in China has been a cause for concern for China's Communist officials. Some types of *qigong* have become pseudo-religions and incorporate deep philosophical and lifestyle teachings. Most famously, falun gong (a.k.a. falun dafa), which is a form of *qigong* that was introduced in China in 1992, has been particularly vilified by the Chinese government and has been banned from the country since 1999.

ACUPUNCTURE

To most Westerners who aren't familiar with it, acupuncture must seem like such a strange treatment. I mean, sticking a bunch of needles into your body to *alleviate* pain? Seems a little paradoxical. But people in China have used acupuncture for thousands of years. Hieroglyphs suggest that variations of acupuncture have been around since the Shang Dynasty (1600–1100 B.C.E.), maybe even earlier.

Acupuncture works on the same principles as other forms of traditional Chinese medicine. The insertion of the needles into certain pressure points (called meridians) on the body helps manage *qi* flow. Acupuncture works to unblock congested *qi* and boosts the body's ability to heal itself. The needles themselves are very thin, making them fairly painless upon insertion. According to the Acupuncture Foundation of Canada, this treatment can help with a number of ailments, including migraines, back pain, tennis elbow, whiplash, Crohn's disease, diarrhea, asthma, depression and menopausal symptoms.

Acupuncture has gained wide acceptance in North America over the past few decades. As of the early 21st century, the provinces of British Columbia, Alberta and Québec regulate acupuncture, and Ontario started to regulate the process in 2005. Many acupuncture practitioners, including those in the Chinese Medicine and Acupuncture Association of Canada, which was established in 1984, welcome regulation because they believe it lends legitimacy to the traditional Chinese practice.

Regulation is also a way to protect patients. As acupuncture's popularity grew in Canada with the arrival of more immigrants and the overall increased interest in Eastern and alternative medicine, so did the number of acupuncture schools. Some programs require students to complete three to five years of training before they can practise acupuncture. Public universities such as McMaster University in Hamilton, Ontario, also offer acupuncture training. But in provinces without regulations, the fear is that anyone can take a two-day course, pronounce themselves to be an acupuncture specialist and start turning people into human porcupines.

In British Columbia today, a province with the second largest Chinese population in Canada that regulates both traditional Chinese medicine and acupuncture, this treatment is very much a part of mainstream health. In 2007, the province added acupuncture to its Medical Service Plan, at an additional cost of about $22 million each year. "Acupuncture is recognized worldwide as a safe and effective way to treat or manage a variety of health conditions," said George Abbott, the province's health minister at the time.

Acupuncture was also fittingly part of the athletes' medical services at the Beijing Olympic Games in 2008. And when thousands of athletes arrived in Vancouver for the 2010 Olympic Winter Games, acupuncturists were made available to them in the medical facilities. Some high-profile athletes to have used acupuncture include speed skater Kevin Overland, from Kitchener, Ontario, and NHL hockey legend Jaromír Jágr.

Tea

Better to be deprived of food for three days, than tea for one.
—ancient Chinese proverb

Arguably the most commonly consumed Chinese medicinal product is tea. It has been brewed for thousands of years, enjoyed by Westerners for centuries and experienced a massive marketing resurgence during the early 21st century as people became more convinced of its potential health benefits. As you may remember from earlier chapters, tea was China's key export for centuries. It remains an important aspect of Chinese culture, and the act of drinking it is often included in special occasions such as weddings or New Years' celebrations.

The origin of tea is shrouded in mythology. Some Chinese believed that Buddha himself drank the first cup of tea. Others credit an emperor named Shennong with discovering it some 5000 years ago when some tea leaves flew into the water he was boiling. If this is true, then green tea would certainly be in the company of penicillin, brandy and gravity as one of the world's most awesome accidental discoveries. Whatever its origin, most researchers seem to agree that the Chinese first cultivated green tea around 2700 B.C.E. From the beginning, tea was seen as a medicinal substance, found helpful for digestion, cleansing and remaining alert.

It wasn't until the Han Dynasty (206 B.C.E. to 220 C.E.) that tea drinking was normalized as an everyday beverage. It became associated with intellectual activities, such as discussion and debate, and was preferred to wine by some. During the Song Dynasty (960 C.E. to 1269 C.E.) tea became more entrenched in rituals and ceremony. It's believed that Japanese Buddhist monks visited China during the Song era and returned to Japan with tea. Green tea has since became a major symbol synonymous with Japan's cultural identity, along with bushido, Shinto and eventually, Pikachu of Pokémon fame.

Tea drinking didn't spread to Europe until around the 17th century, when trading with China began in earnest. The British later introduced tea culture to India. Canada received its first taste of tea through the Hudson's Bay Company in the early 18th century. We've been loving it ever since. In 2005, the per capita consumption of tea in Canada was 69.98 litres (280 cups) per Canadian, an increase of 43 percent from 1996 when it was 48.9 litres, according to the Tea Association of Canada. That means that an astounding seven billion cups of tea are filled and consumed each year.

With so many teacups being drained and refilled every year, tea has become big business in Canada. In 2005, the tea market in Canada was worth approximately $305 million. Coffee, which originated in North Africa, is still king among Canadians—over 15 billion cups are consumed every year—but tea products, especially herbal iced tea drinks, were one of the fastest growing beverage markets in Canada between 2005 and 2010.

The culture, recreation and appreciation of tea has grown immensely. Although people in Canada have enjoyed the English tradition of high tea for quite some time, Canadians have now also learned to embrace the more Chinese-style of drinking loose-leaf tea (not in bags) and leaving out the milk and sugar.

The Chinese tend to think of tea in the same way that Europeans approach wine—each variety of tea has distinctive characteristics that give it a flavour and aroma that can be enjoyed on their own or used to complement food. Tea-appreciation societies and classes and workshops on how to distinguish different types of tea have popped up all over the country.

More people are also turning to tea as careers. In 2007, George Brown College in Toronto introduced North America's first professional tea sommelier program. It's much like the school's wine sommelier course—students learn about the basic components of tea, its growth and production, the different flavour profiles and traditional cupping and serving procedures. The course then moves into mixology and pairing tea with food. Graduates of this program are certified to work as tea buyers and tasters for retail stores, restaurants and hotels. For example, the luxurious Park Hyatt hotel in Chicago employs a tea sommelier who is responsible for handling expensive teas, including a Chinese green tea from 1985 that costs more than US$300 per pot.

"There is as much detail and depth as wine," chief instructor Bill Kamula told the *Vancouver Sun* in 2009. "The claim is made there are 9000 green teas in China. I would challenge the French to come up with 9000 wines."

So which teas complement which foods? Well, it helps to understand the basic varieties of tea and how they differ. Chinese teas can be separated into several groups. They include black (leaves fermented before heating), green (the most popular form, unfermented), oolong (partially fermented, kind of a cross between black and green), and white (processed but barely oxidized). Within these categories of teas are hundreds of unique varieties that come from China's different regions.

Here are some of the more intriguing varieties:

Aged *Tie Guan Yin*

These oolong tea leaves are picked from 300-year-old trees by Wuyi Mountain in southeastern China's Fujian province. This rare tea is smoked over a fire for a total of

80 hours, little by little, over a period of more than 12 years. It's like the single-malt scotch of teas. A one-kilogram bag of this stuff could set you back well over $200.

IMPERIAL PU-ERH

This tea comes from the border of China and Vietnam. Unlike most teas, which are processed and released immediately, this type is fermented and stored for about 15 years, which gives it a rich, full taste and earthy flavour.

TAI PING HOU KWEI

This green tea with a slightly sweet taste hails from Tai Ping Country of Huei Province in an area known as Monkey Hill. The large, tender tea leaves are so delicate that they're picked strictly during the fog-filled mornings of spring.

MONKEY-PICKED TEA

That's right. Some varieties of Chinese tea are grown so high up that people have trained monkeys to shimmy up trees and scamper across mountainsides to collect the leaves. It has been a tradition for centuries that apparently continues to this day in one or two remote villages in China.

If you're eating something rich and creamy, goat cheese perhaps, then a tea sommelier may suggest pairing it with jasmine tea, a green tea that's grassy, crisp and fragrant. A meal of dim sum usually features oily, fried items that match well with *pu-erh* tea, a bold, slightly bitter variety that stands up to heavier foods. *Pu-erh* is the only Chinese tea that's fermented after production, so its flavour changes character and gains complexity with time, like fine wine. White teas, milder in flavour, tend to go best with sweeter foods such as cakes, tarts and waffles.

HEALTH CLAIMS

Interest in tea culture in Canada grew significantly in the early 21st century, but the biggest explanation for tea's rise in popularity, especially unfermented green tea, has to do with the myriad health benefits that drinking green tea supposedly yields. The Chinese have been drinking it for centuries as a health beverage, and recent scientific research has suggested it may indeed offer some health advantages.

Green tea is rich in catechins and other polyphenols, compounds believed to have antioxidant properties. Antioxidants, as you've no doubt gleaned from countless commercials and magazine ads, destroy free radicals and help reduce oxidation in the body. Free radicals and cellular oxidation leads to cell damage, which is linked to the onset of cancer. Polyphenols are also found in red wine, although—unlike with tea—it's difficult to drink more than two or three glasses of it over lunch without attracting unwanted attention.

Green tea, on the other hand, is now being put into everything. Iced-tea companies offer green tea versions of their products, and green tea powder (or *matcha*) is mixed into smoothies and frozen yogurt. Green tea has also found its way into moisturizers and hair products. Green tea pills are another popular supplement.

Recent studies have indicated that green tea can reduce cholesterol and heart disease, lower systolic and diastolic blood pressure, prevent glaucoma, ease dandruff, normalize hormonal levels, and may also help weight loss by increasing metabolism.

Most of these studies have followed small sample sizes. Larger green tea studies have produced mixed results. One study in China, published in 2002 and involving 18,000 men, found that regular green tea drinkers were half as likely to develop stomach or esophageal cancer as men who didn't drink tea. However, a previous study of over 100,000 people between the ages of 55 and 69 found no link between drinking tea and preventing cancer.

But while the jury's still out on the health properties of green tea, the popular vote is in. Tea is one Chinese delight that Canadians will pour into a cup and use to make a toast to good health (apparently, over seven billion times per year).

Chapter Thirteen

Sports

Growing up, I was never particularly adept at sports. I generally dreaded gym class. Sure, I liked basketball, but I had the leaping ability of an orange traffic cone. Despite my living in Canada, playing hockey never appealed to me, probably because of my dubious balance on land, never mind on skates. My mediocre-at-best hand-eye coordination also discouraged me from participating in most sports involving small, bouncing balls that would likely end up smacking me in the face. (I'm still haunted by memories of one especially humiliating game of table tennis.)

The only sports I had any success in were the martial arts—taekwondo and karate, mainly. That is so unfortunately stereotypical, but when it comes to punching and kicking air, I'm Michael Jordan.

See, it didn't matter if I did poorly at other, more Western sports. It was almost expected. "Hey, it's OK, you're Chinese," one of my more athletically gifted peers would tell me after I'd fumble a football or something. "You guys are good in school."

Don't get me wrong. There are Chinese Canadian athletes everywhere, excelling in all kinds of sports at all different levels. But for the most part, the Chinese don't really come to mind when discussing Canadian sports history. Who are the most important Canadian athletes in history? The Great One, Wayne Gretzky, would be on that list. Terry Fox ran over 5000 kilometres across this country after losing one leg to cancer. Rick Hansen, a wheelchair-bound paraplegic athlete was so inspirational, he became the subject of the hit song "St. Elmo's Fire (Man in Motion)" by David Foster. You'd also have to include Bobby Orr, Nancy Greene...the list goes on.

If you ask most people who's on that list, it's unlikely a Chinese Canadian athlete would immediately pop up. To this day, not too many Chinese Canadians play at the very highest level of this country's most popular sports.

But there are actually many great Chinese Canadian athletes in our country's history. You have to dig a little deeper to find them, but their stories are an important part of the Chinese Canadian narrative. These athletes defied the expectations and served as inspirations for a Chinese community in Canada that was still searching for acceptance and respect. The first Chinese Canadian sports stars had a lot more at stake than just winning or losing a game—they carried the weight of an entire community's hopes and aspirations.

Quene Yip, Vancouver's Soccer Legend

Yip was born in Vancouver's Chinatown on November 6, 1905. Quene (pronounced "Queenie") was the 16th of 23 children. He had 18 brothers and four sisters. His father,

Yip Sang, a prominent local businessman, had four wives. The Yips were considered the largest family in all of Vancouver, and if Quene and his siblings had been born in the 21st century, they would probably have been given a reality television show on the TLC television network.

Quene showed athletic promise early in his life. He became a dominant track and field star, winning the individual championship at the city's inter–high school track and field meet in 1925. Quene even defeated Percy Williams, the Vancouver-born runner who would later become a national hero for bringing home double gold for Canada by winning the 100-metre and 200-metre sprints at the 1928 Olympic Games in Amsterdam.

In the fall of 1925, Quene was one of the first Chinese Canadians to gain acceptance into the University of British Columbia (UBC). It was a proud moment for his father, a respected leader in the Chinese community who helped establish the city's Chinese Benevolent Association and strongly believed in education.

But you couldn't really blame Quene if he had more than just books on his mind. He quickly established himself as the university's finest soccer player. Playing the centre-forward position, he was exceptionally strong, had excellent footwork and led his teams unselfishly. The city's *Province* newspaper described him as "clever with his head and feet, and possessing great speed. He is a terror to opposing goalkeepers." Pretty soon, many observers considered him to be the top soccer player in all of British Columbia.

His career at UBC officially lasted only one stellar year. He transferred to Queen's University in Kingston, Ontario, where he stayed until 1929. While at Queen's, he played centre-forward for the school's team, earning more praise and press clippings.

After moving back to Vancouver, he rejoined the city's Chinese Students Athletic Club, a sports group with which he had played prior to and during his university career. The Chinese community gave the team immense support, and it was said the streets of Chinatown were virtually empty every time they played because everyone had gone to watch the game. These local players were the first all–Chinese Canadian soccer team in history, making them heroes to the Chinese community.

And these Chinese players were good. Really good. They regularly pulled off wins against top competition from around the province and took home league championships. But their biggest, and most enduring, victory came in 1933. That was year the Chinese students club, led by Quene, took it all the way and won the province's highly coveted Mainland Cup.

Chinatown exploded with celebration. The day after the milestone event, Chinese community leaders declared the day a holiday. The young men were honoured in an open-car parade and were cheered on by thousands. Restaurant owners gave out dim sum, while musicians played on the streets. The win was a win for every Chinese person in Canada at the time. After years of being treated as inferiors by other Canadians, it must have felt good to prove to the entire province that the Chinese could rise to the occasion and compete with the very best, if at least in soccer. And if they did it once, they could do it again.

This victory proved to be the defining moment of Quene's prolific soccer career. After his playing days were over, he settled down with his wife, Victoria, and worked as a chemist and writer. They had a family and stayed together until the winter of their days.

Until he died, in March 1994 at age 88, Quene Yip remained Vancouver's most celebrated Chinese Canadian soccer star, in the same city where he was born. Friends remembered him as a man with strong morals and someone who saw the importance of good sportsmanship. After all, good sportsmanship, he said in 1939, enabled people to feel "happiness within and radiate happiness among those with whom we associate."

Quene was inducted into British Columbia's Sports Hall of Fame in 1998, honoured as one of the province's pioneer sports stars.

Larry Kwong—The NHL's First Chinese

The story of Larry Kwong, the Chinese Canadian who broke the NHL's colour barrier, is often overlooked, which is somewhat surprising for a hockey-mad nation such as Canada.

Larry was born on June 17, 1923, to immigrant parents who ran a corner store in Vernon, British Columbia. He was one of 15 children.

Young Larry fell in love with hockey while listening to Foster Hewitt call games over the radio in the family's apartment above the shop. They lived in Vernon's small Chinatown, which no longer exists.

He loved the game so much that he and his friends often hiked six or seven kilometres from their homes up to Mud Lake, which had the only available ice during winter.

Larry played midget hockey for the Vernon Hydrophones and immediately showed tremendous promise. "Oh, exceptional around the net," recalled former teammate George Dobie years later in an interview with *Insider's Edge* magazine. "Exceptional. He could put it up in that top corner better than they do in the NHL now. His hands were quick. Good stickhandler. His skating was perfect. They couldn't touch him. He was too quick."

Larry's speedy game earned him the nickname "China Clipper," a reference to the first airplane that delivered mail from China to Canada. The same nickname was later bestowed upon Normie Kwong (no relation to Larry), a Chinese Canadian football player we'll see in this chapter soon enough. Kwong and Dobie helped their team win several championships. Despite the Hydrophones' success, Larry still faced discrimination in his own hometown. There were times when barbers refused to give him a haircut.

Larry's skills on the ice earned him a place on the Smoke Eaters hockey squad in the town of Trail. But he didn't find much acceptance there either. Every player on the Smoke Eaters was given a job at Cominico, a local mining and smelting operation. Every player except Larry. "They wouldn't give me a job, even though I was Canadian, because I was Chinese," he recalled in the *Vernon Morning Star* newspaper in 2009. Larry focused on improving his game and taking it to the next level. He joined the New York Rangers' farm team, the Rovers, for the 1946–47 season. He played in a total of 47 games, scoring 19 goals and 37 points.

The big league took notice. The following year, Larry was called up to the Rangers to play against the Montréal Canadiens (led by the legendary Rocket Richard) in the city's old Forum. On March 13, 1948, he donned a blue Rangers hockey sweater bearing the number 11 and sat on the bench. The first period went by. He sat there, clutching his stick. Then the second period ended. Finally, during the third period, his coach tapped him on the shoulder. Larry hopped over the boards. As soon as his skates touched the ice, he made history by becoming the first Chinese Canadian to play in the NHL.

His shift lasted about one minute, and so did his major league career. He skated back to the bench, never to return to NHL play.

Although Larry's time in the big leagues turned out to be short, his journey to the NHL made headlines everywhere. New York's large Chinese community was elated by his appearance on the ice. Back in his hometown of Vernon, where he once couldn't even get a haircut, the local newspaper proclaimed him as the town's "most famous hockey player and ambassador." The paper said NHL stardom "couldn't happen to a nicer fellow or a more sportsmanlike player. Vernon can well be proud of their representative in hockey's big time."

Larry's moment in the spotlight was both a blessing and a bane. He did manage to attain his childhood dream of suiting up for an NHL team. Yet he realized the New York Rangers had only been interested in playing him as something of a publicity stunt. At that point in time, the NHL wasn't ready for a Chinese player and never gave him a chance to prove he belonged there. He was at the top for only 60 seconds—that must have been so hard to live with.

Larry spent the rest of his hockey career in the minor leagues, including stints in Troy, Ohio; Trois-Rivières, Québec; and Nottingham, England. When he retired, he worked as a tennis and hockey coach in Europe before returning home to run the family grocery store.

Larry's groundbreaking appearance on the ice preceded Fred Sasakamoose, the first Canadian Aboriginal to play in the NHL, by five years, and preceded Willie O'Ree, the first African Canadian in the NHL, by a decade.

Both Sasakamoose and O'Ree went on to have longer NHL careers.

As the decades went by following Larry's monumental moment on the ice, the story of the NHL's first Chinese player faded into memory. But in the early 21st century, some first-, second- and third-generation Asian Canadians learned of Larry's legacy and, inspired by his story, made it their mission to get him recognized for his contribution to Canadian sports history. The Larry Kwong Appreciation Society, led by Chad Soon, a teacher and hockey fan from British Columbia, contacted dozens of NHL teams, radio stations, media organizations and even trading card companies in an effort to celebrate Larry's story.

The group's campaign paid off. On March 20, 2008, six decades after Larry's single NHL appearance, the Calgary Flames honoured him with a video tribute during a game against the Colorado Avalanche. His story was also recounted on CBC Radio and in the *Globe and Mail* newspaper.

Larry Kwong was allowed to live his dream for exactly one minute, and it's incredible to think that one minute of an entire NHL career could echo throughout history.

NORMAN KWONG—THE CFL'S FIRST CHINESE

There is perhaps no Chinese Canadian athlete more decorated than CFL legend "Normie" Kwong. Few Canadian athletes of any ethnicity can boast the accolades, awards and respect he has received over the years.

He was born in Calgary in 1929 to Charles and Lily Kwong. One of six children, Normie and his family lived fairly close to the city's Chinatown. The children attended Chinese school in Chinatown, and, although Normie was passionate about sports from an early age, in secondary school he discovered that he had a special talent for football.

After playing for Western Canada High School, he found himself, at age 18, invited to join the Calgary Stampeders as a halfback in 1948. He was a mere 5 feet 7 inches tall and weighed about 170 pounds, but he was a powerful athlete. Normie went on to have an incredible career that surpassed all expectations.

His CFL journey kicked off with a bang. During his rookie year, he broke two records: he became the first Chinese Canadian to play in the CFL and the youngest player to ever win the Grey Cup. Early in his career, his speedy play saw him inherit the nickname "China Clipper" from Larry Kwong.

Normie played with the Stampeders for three seasons before being traded to the Edmonton Eskimos to play fullback. While in Edmonton, he blossomed into an all-star athlete. In 11 CFL seasons, he rushed for more than 9000 yards and scored 93 touchdowns. He earned the All-Canadian Fullback Award five times and the Schenley Award as the Most Outstanding Canadian in 1955 and 1956. In 1955, he was named as Canada's Outstanding Male Athlete of the Year. By the time Normie retired in 1960, he held over 30 CFL records. In addition to his individual accolades, he helped his team win three Grey Cup championships between 1954 and 1956. Whew!

During his superlative career, Normie became an immensely popular figure within the Chinese Canadian community. Award-winning Chinese Canadian writer Wayson Choy remembered following Normie's games and how his Grey Cup victories would spark joyous celebrations in Chinatown. "He was like a superhero," Choy said.

Players and supporters of the Calgary Stampeders celebrate their 1948 Grey Cup championship. Norman Kwong, the CFL's first Chinese player, is on the right, as indicated by the white arrow.

⁂

Normie was inducted into the Canadian Football Hall of Fame in 1969, the Canadian Sports Hall of Fame in 1975 and the Alberta Sports Hall of Fame in 1987. In November 2006, he was named one of the CFL's Top 50 players of the modern era by Canadians sports network TSN, an honour few of his contemporaries received.

After retiring from the game, Normie put his energies into business, mainly in selling commercial real estate. But he wasn't out of the sports landscape for long. From 1988 to 1999, he returned to the CFL team with which he had started his pro career, the Stampeders, serving as president and general manager. He also became a co-owner of the Calgary Flames between 1980 and 1994. The Flames won the Stanley Cup in 1989, making Normie one of the few Canadians to have won both the Grey Cup and Lord Stanley's award.

In 1988, he was awarded the Order of Canada and received a knighthood from Queen Elizabeth in 2005. At the Canadian Embassy in Beijing, the fitness centre is named the Normie Kwong Gymnasium in his honour. In 2005, Prime Minister Paul Martin appointed him Alberta's 16th lieutenant-governor, making him the first Asian Canadian to hold such a position. In February 2010, with his term ending, he delivered his final throne speech.

"It has been my honour to serve Albertans as lieutenant-governor over these past five years," Kwong said. "This job has been the highlight of a rewarding career that took many unexpected turns. No one could be as surprised as I am that my road brought me to where it did."

A few days after Normie made his final speech as lieutenant-governor, I had the opportunity to speak with him about his astonishing life. The following are excerpts from our interview.

Q: Did you know much about your parents coming to Canada?

Not a lot. They were from Canton, I think maybe 90 percent of Chinese people came from Canton. You know, they were here years before I arrived, of course, being born in 1929. They were married in Victoria after they arrived through an arranged marriage.

It was tough for them when they first got over here. Of course, when my dad came over, they were still wearing pigtails and that, you see. So they were made fun of when they went to work, and most of them had to work at the mines, doing menial jobs, the cooking and things like that.

Q: What was life like in Calgary during the 1930s and 1940s?

My parents owned a grocery store with another Chinese family in the same neighbourhood—we were the only Chinese in the area and we grew up slightly different than everybody else. Most of the people in my neighbourhood were Germans and Russians. [The Germans] were kind of feeling a little bit discriminated against because it was during the war years. They always used to say they were Russians, rather than Germans. It was not an easy childhood, but a good childhood.

Q: Do you remember facing much discrimination?

Well, in my lifetime…there's been a huge, huge cultural change as far as the attitude towards Chinese go. In the early days, we were such a small part of the population that we were a minority and treated that way.

My oldest brother and sister encountered more discrimination than we did later on. But I can remember them being called names and my older brother being picked on, and myself wanting to go help him fight or something. Of course, I was too small then.

I used to play softball or fastball and I used to play on a team, and we used to go play in the smaller towns. Sometimes in the smaller towns, where there weren't any Chinese families, you'd get called names and things like that because they weren't familiar with Chinese people. But most of my teammates rallied behind me and we kind of battled through.

I don't think in my lifetime I ever encountered any real outright, really bad discrimination. There was always an element of discrimination, only because [people in the smaller towns] weren't familiar with any Chinese people.

Q: You were a Canadian-born football star in your local community, yet you weren't considered a Canadian citizen until after 1945. How did it feel when you finally gained citizenship?

I was only in high school, and high school juniors didn't really recognize the fact. But when it finally happened, I knew my dad was especially proud of being able to be a Canadian. He made a special point of keeping his citizenship papers in his store and showing them to people, showing them to his customers when they came in. He was very proud to be Canadian.

Q: Did you realize how popular you were in the Chinese Canadian community?

Kind of, but not really—the Chinatown in Calgary wasn't a huge population. And they didn't make a special deal 'cause they knew our family so well. But going to other cities...I know that in Vancouver and different places they were quite proud of the fact that I was Chinese Canadian. Well, it was good because I got along better with girls that way. [Laughs.] No, it was fine. It was just an area of distinction for me.

Q: Looking back, what are your fondest memories?

In sports, I think the fact that I was chosen Most Outstanding Canadian a couple of years in a row and also winning those Grey Cups was always a big thing in my life. And, I actually met my wife [Mary] through football, only because the team went to Vancouver and my cousins took me to this party and that's where I met her.

People like Quene Yip, Larry Kwong and Normie Kwong paved the way for future Chinese Canadian athletes.

They certainly had the odds stacked against them, living in a time when ethnic tensions often ran high and many Chinese were not allowed to participate in sports leagues or clubs. We can only wonder what other young Chinese Canadians of their generations could have achieved in sports had they received the support of the wider community and been given a level playing field.

In more recent decades, Chinese Canadians have integrated well into mainstream Canadian society and enjoy playing the same sports as everybody else. Many have found success at both the amateur and professional levels. Who could forget Lori Fung, the brilliant Vancouver-born Olympian who dazzled in her rhythmic gymnastics routines at the 1984 Los Angeles Games. The sport was new to the Olympics, and she won the first-ever gold. A few years later, Chan-on Goh, a Beijing-born dancer who had immigrated to Canada with her family, became the first Chinese Canadian principal dancer for the National Ballet of Canada.

Younger generations of Chinese Canadians born in the late 20th century are also making their presence felt and competing at some of the highest levels, including figure skater Patrick Chan, snowboarder Alexa Loo, hockey player Chris Beckford-Tseu and CFL centre Bryan Chiu.

OLD WORLD SPORTS

Of course, with so many Chinese living in Canada, it was only a matter of time before traditional Chinese sports caught on with non-Chinese. While they don't enjoy the same level of popularity as, say, hockey or curling, these sports are attracting Canadians interested in new physical and mental challenges. And when you think of the Chinese sports that have become a significant part of Canada's sports landscape, dragon boat racing and *wushu*—more often known as kung fu—immediately come to mind.

Dragon Boat Racing

Canadians have a long, proud tradition of boating and sailing, from Nova Scotia's legendary *Bluenose* to Olympian rower Silken Laumann. So it's probably no surprise that the Chinese import of dragon boat racing has taken root in Canada and grown quite spectacularly.

Dragon boats vary in size and shape, but what they have in common is that they all generally look totally awesome. These canoe-like boats are sleek, painted with kaleidoscopic colours and feature a traditional Chinese dragon head at the front. The crew sizes can be as small as 10 or as large as 50, most of them paddlers, while one drummer pounds out a primal metronome beat.

Dragon boats are believed to have originated in China more than 2000 years ago, although as with many Chinese inventions, the exact circumstances of their creation are unclear. People in some parts of China have passed on the popular myth that dragon boat racing was born when a well-respected official of the empire who had long fought against corruption threw himself into the Miluo River after tragic events led to his exile. The official, named Qu Yuan, was much loved by the common people, and several men took off in rowboats to find his body. They brought along drummers to scare away the fish and evil spirits and threw *zong zi* (rice dumplings) into the water to distract water creatures from eating his body. The practice of taking boats out into the water and beating drums became an annual tradition—on the fifth day of the fifth lunar month (usually early June by our calendar), people gather by the water for the dragon boat festival, *Duanwu Jie*.

Canada has a unique history with dragon boat racing. As early at 1945, after the end of World War II, officials from China were in Vancouver discussing the possibility of the city hosting the first dragon boat race outside of Asia. People in China considered Vancouver the gateway to North America, and the idea was to hold the dragon boat race as part of the city's 60th anniversary.

For whatever reason, the dragon boat race didn't happen until Vancouver's 100th anniversary. The city was hosting Expo '86 at the time, which must have been some party. Six authentic dragon boats were donated to the city, and the Chinese Cultural Centre Dragon Boat Association was created to help organize the first races in Canada using traditional boats. In subsequent years, many other Canadian cities, from Regina to Ottawa and even Banff, began featuring annual dragon boat festivals.

Ten years after the 1986 race, the International Dragon Boat Federation, the sport's world governing body, chose Vancouver to host the world championships. Toronto had the same honour a decade later, marking the 20th anniversary of dragon boat racing in Canada.

The ancient Chinese sport of dragon boat racing has become a cherished activity for many people because it's physically demanding and team-oriented. But the sport has found a special place among breast cancer survivors. In 1998, a *Canadian Medical Journal* article by sports physician Don McKenzie, from the University of British Columbia, suggested that dragon boat racing was beneficial for survivors of breast cancer.

Dr. McKenzie studied the effect of dragon boat racing on a group of survivors and found that their physical strength increased because of the repetitive upper-body movements of rowing, and because there's no weight-bearing movement, the risk of injury was minimized. He also observed that the women gained a better sense of well-being during and after chemotherapy and radiation treatments because of the team support. McKenzie's research partially explains the large number of breast cancer survivor teams that compete in dragon boat races around the world every year.

For many cities in Canada, dragon boat festivals rank among their top tourist attractions.

COMPETITIVE *WUSHU* (KUNG FU)

OK, if there's one sport that Chinese people are stereotypically known for (besides ping pong), it has to be kung fu. And most Chinese are fine with that. Kung fu, or *wushu* as it's known in modern China, is part of the Chinese identity. This old-world sport plays a huge role in traditional Chinese folklore and modern popular culture. Many Chinese arts, from opera to lion dancing, involve acrobatic fighting moves. Even Chinese traditional medicine, as we've seen with tai chi and *qigong*, incorporate martial arts techniques and philosophies.

And, of course, martial arts play a starring role in many Chinese movies, from historical epics about wars and warlords to Hong Kong–style action films chock-full of stunts, explosions and dramatic hand-to-hand duels in the rain.

There are many styles of martial arts in China, and they all fall under the umbrella term of *wushu*. Chinese martial arts can be traced back nearly 4000 years to the Xia Dynasty. Soldiers and warriors developed various forms of hand-to-hand combat, sometimes involving weapons. The Shaolin monks are credited with creating the first institutionalized systems of martial arts in China. As a matter of self-defence, the monks developed styles of boxing, sword-fighting and forms based on the animals of Asia, such as the Eagle Claw, Praying Mantis and Monkey styles. Maybe if kung fu had been created in Canada, we'd have cool martial arts' moves like the Goose Grip or the Snowshoe Hare Headbutt. That would definitely liven up the hockey fights.

The martial arts evolved in China over thousands of years, leading to an amazing and diverse number of styles. In 1949, after the founding of the People's Republic, the Chinese government recognized the primacy of kung fu in Chinese culture and moved to nationalize martial arts by calling it *wushu* and introducing a sport competition system.

Few Chinese learn kung fu in Shaolin temples anymore, but hundreds of millions are in state-sponsored *wushu* academies. *Wushu* is China's most popular national sport, and some competitive *wushu* practitioners spend countless hours perfecting their art. Action star Jet Li first gained prominence in China by becoming a national *wushu* champion. Ray Park, the British stunt actor best known for playing the stealthy, acrobatic and uber-evil Darth Maul in *Star Wars: The Phantom Menace,* started to train in *wushu* at the age of seven.

Like Japanese karate and Korean taekwondo before it, *wushu* spread across the globe largely through the introduction of competition. Sport *wushu* is divided into two forms: *taolu,* the performance of non-contact, choreographed routines, and *sanshou,* which is full-contact freestyle fighting.

Taolu competitors can do set routines or opt to display their own mishmash of different kung-fu styles. The forms are judged on the degree of difficulty of the movements and techniques. There are also duo routines and weapons categories.

Sanshou is an exciting form of sparring that involves punching, kicking and grappling. It's full contact, but there are rules (such as no striking the back of the head) to protect fighters in international competition. The combatants generally wear head gear, a chest protector and gloves during the bout.

Competitive *wushu* remains a niche sport in North America in the early 21st century, but it has grown by leaps and bounds and is rapidly gaining popularity. Wushu Canada, a national organization promoting the sport in this country, had more than 5000 members in 2010 and 250 athletes in active competition.

In 2009, Toronto became the first Canadian city, and the second in North America, to host the World Wushu Championships, the biennial competition organized by the International Wushu Federation. It's the World Cup of *wushu*, which began in Beijing, China, in 1991. The six-day event in Toronto drew more than 600 athletes from 72 countries and an estimated 50,000 spectators.

Although competitive martial arts in general has always lagged behind other spectator sports such as baseball or basketball in North America, mixed martial arts, as epitomized by the Ultimate Fighting Championship (UFC), the biggest mixed martial arts promotion in the world, has been quickly closing the gap, especially since the late 1990s. Once referred to as "human cockfighting" by U.S. Senator (and presidential candidate) John McCain, professional mixed martial arts fighting, which evolved from its no-holds-barred roots to include some rules and regulations to protect the fighters, has become a mainstream spectator sport.

And there are few places in the world that mixed martial arts has grown faster than in Canada. A national poll in

2009 found that 20 percent of Canadian adults regularly watched ultimate fighting events. UFC president Dana White once called Canada the "mecca" of his sport. Montréal's Georges St. Pierre, a UFC champion and one of the mixed martial arts' most famous fighters, was named Canada's Athlete of the Year for 2008 and 2009 by the national sports network Sportsnet.

The exploding popularity of mixed martial arts can only mean a wider interest in competitive *wushu* and Chinese martial arts history. After all, White once credited a well-known Chinese man for being "the grandfather of mixed martial arts"; he was talking about the "Little Dragon," Bruce Lee.

CHAPTER FOURTEEN

ARTS AND ENTERTAINMENT

There's no doubt that Canada boasts a proud legacy of producing great artists, performers and entertainers: from the beautiful landscapes painted by the Group of Seven, to Margaret Atwood's enigmatic, provocative writing, to the eternal comedic talents of SCTV and Rick Mercer. And there's also no doubt that Chinese Canadians have contributed greatly to this country's art history.

The emergence of Chinese Canadian art and artists began in Chinatown. The early Chinese immigrants brought with them their passion for traditional performing arts and entertainment such as Cantonese-language opera and music. They also introduced other kinds of culturally important art to Canada, including Chinese calligraphy and Chinese-style painting that both utilize brushes dipped in coloured ink, not oil paint.

Opera in particular played a hugely important role in early Chinese Canadian communities. Chinese opera is a dazzling combination of singing, elaborate costumes, storytelling (usually involving themes of war, love and tragedy) and acrobatic martial arts–based tumbling. Some of the first Chinese artistic and social groups in Canada were opera-appreciation clubs. By the 1870s, three such clubs had been established in Victoria. Chinatown's merchant class helped to support these groups because they saw how important they were in bringing the community together socially. A clipping from the *British Colonist* newspaper described the construction of three Cantonese opera theatres in the 1880s, one of which reportedly sat up to 800 patrons.

Professional Chinese opera touring companies from San Francisco and Hong Kong were frequently invited to perform full-length programs in the halls and theatres of Canada's Chinatowns. From the 1920s onward, 78 rpm vinyl recordings of popular opera songs were available. Eventually, the Chinese Canadian community grew large enough to provide the necessary talent and personnel to produce Chinese opera. Some of the earliest local opera associations, including Jin Wah Sing and the Ching Won Musical Society, were founded in Vancouver during the early 1930s.

Growing alongside the opera clubs were musical instrument groups. People gathered and played traditional Chinese instruments like the *dizi* (bamboo flute), the *qinqin* (longneck lute) and the *gaohu* (fiddle). Unlike opera, which required singers and actors to learn melodies and lyrics through notation, an amateur instrumentalist could learn to play without having to read music. It was easy to form ensembles, and although little documentation

Traditional Chinese opera performers put on a show at Moose Hall in Edmonton, Alberta, in 1931. Opera was one of the most popular pastimes for Chinese Canadian communities.

exists from the early groups in British Columbia, they were apparently very popular and performed at Chinese festivals and banquets. As the years progressed, it wasn't unusual for Chinese ensembles to include Western instruments such as the guitar, saxophone or double bass.

Chinese opera in Canada lulled a bit between the 1940s and 1960s, as older Chinese Canadians passed away and Canadian-born Chinese, who were more integrated than the previous generation, showed more interest in Western entertainment such as movies. But the immigration wave after the mid-1960s brought in many people from Hong Kong who breathed new life back into the opera and music societies. Chinese communities across Canada established schools that taught traditional performing arts to newer generations of Chinese Canadians.

In the early 21st century, Chinese opera continued to be a popular pastime, especially in Toronto and Vancouver, which boast the largest home-grown opera groups. The recent emergence of China and the increase of immigration from mainland China has also sparked the growth of Beijing-style theatre in Canada, which is similar to Cantonese opera (and enjoys a equally long history in the motherland) but is performed in Mandarin.

Of course, with so many Chinese now living in Canada, other non-traditional forms of Chinese music have become popular as well. Cantonese- and Mandarin-language pop music (referred to as "Cantopop" and "Mandopop," respectively) have significant followings in Canada, especially among Chinese Canadian youth. The music is much like Western pop music—think choreographed dance moves and catchy tunes performed by great-looking, though sometimes dubiously talented, youngsters in edgy fashion—except the lyrics are in Chinese.

Pop singers from China, Hong Kong and Taiwan often tour in North America and regularly sell out stadium shows in cities with large Chinese populations. The global reach of Chinese pop music, largely as a result of the mass Chinese migrations of the late 20th century, was the subject of a *TIME* magazine article in 2001:

> Cantopop stars are mobbed in Beijing and Taipei, in London and Las Vegas. [In 2000], veteran mesmerizer Leslie Cheung gave a sold-out concert at Caesars Palace, where tickets went for $80 and $238. The same night, half a mile down the Strip, Jackie Chan—yes, he's also a singer—led an all-star music revue that packed the 17,000-seat Garden at the MGM Grand at a top price of $150.

In Canada, the response has been similar. Stars such as Hong Kong actor/singer Jacky Cheung and Taiwan singer-songwriter Jay Chou have played to capacity crowds at the Air Canada Centre in Toronto, where the city's Raptors and Maple Leafs sports franchises play. Veteran prince of Chinese pop Andy Lau has drawn thousands to The Centre in Vancouver, a venue also previously graced by mega acts such as Sting and Tom Jones ("The Voice!").

A particularly fascinating phenomenon is that Canada is now a major supplier of Chinese pop stars to Asia and Chinese communities around the world. As of the early 21st century, several of the biggest Chinese singers and actors were born or raised in Canada, or both, during the 1980s. Their families had come during the Hong Kong exodus, settling in Canada's most populous Chinese communities. As a result, many members of this younger generation of Chinese pop stars are perfectly fluent in both English and various Chinese dialects.

Nicholas Tse, a guitarist and singer with a nonchalant "bad boy" image, grew up in Vancouver and attended the prestigious St. George's boarding school. A Hong Kong music executive heard him singing at a party and signed him to his label. Tse went on to became one of the most recognizable singers and action film stars in Asia. Charlene Choi, born in Vancouver in 1982, later moved to Hong Kong and eventually became a member of the incredibly successful pop-rock band called Twins.

One of most famous Chinese pop stars of the modern era is Edison Chen, born in Vancouver in 1980. He went to Hong Kong to begin a modelling and singing/rapping career but quickly became one of the Asian film industry's biggest young stars. He was even mired in a sex photo scandal in 2008 (a rare event in the Asian entertainment industry) after pictures of him fooling around with some of China's most popular female celebrities were leaked from his laptop. Several other of Asia's most popular stars in the early 21st century are originally from Canada, including singers Kelvin Kwan and Brandon Chang from Toronto and Angela Tong from Montréal.

Chinese Canadians, particularly newer generations, have also been integrated into mainstream Western-style entertainment and performance arts and have created English-language plays, musicals and films that explore Chinese culture, history and Canadian identity. Throughout the 1980s, playwright Winston Kam put on a production called *Bachelor Man,* which explored the Chinese Exclusion Act of 1923. In 1996, Vancouver's Betty Quan staged the play *Mother Tongue* that examined the cultural and generational differences in Chinese Canadian families.

Marty Chan has written several plays, including the cheekily titled *Mom, Dad—I'm Living with a White Girl.* He also hosted a CBC radio series called *Dim Sum Diaries* during the late 1990s. The show dealt with his experiences growing up in the only Chinese family in small-town northern Alberta.

Toronto-based filmmaker Keith Lock has tackled subjects ranging from immigrant students living in Canada *(A Brighter Moon)* to homosexuality within the context of Chinese culture and identity *(Small Pleasures).*

Vancouver-based composer Chan Ka Nin's 2001 opera *Iron Road* took audiences back to the railway days. A few years later, it was adapted into a movie starring several big-name actors, including Tony Leung from Hong Kong and Peter O'Toole and Sam Neil from the UK.

Chinese Canadians continue to make culturally and historically compelling works of film and theatre.

With the proliferation of Asian Canadian arts festivals and organizations, such as the Toronto Reel Asian International Film Festival and Vancouver's Asian Canadian Theatre, Chinese Canadians are finding more avenues than ever to present their unique projects.

Chinese visual artists are a significant part of the Canadian arts community as well. Younger generations have preserved more traditional styles and techniques, ranging from painting, printmaking, sculpture, seal carving and calligraphy to more modern art such as abstract imagery, site installations, photography and video.

Ying Wong, who was born and educated in China, has published several books on Chinese calligraphy and Chinese paintings. Alan Chung Hung, a Vancouver-based artist, is famous for his large public sculptures and was one of the founding members of the Chinese Canadian Visual Arts Society, established in 1983. This society organized the first large-scale exhibit of Chinese Canadian artists in Vancouver in 1994. Fifty artists of contemporary and traditional styles, including fashion designers Simon Chang and Alfred Sung, displayed their work at the exhibit.

In the early 1990s, several artists, such as Ana Chang, Diana Li, Paul Wong and Sharyn Yuen, incorporated a variety of media styles to examine Chinese Canadian identity in a group exhibition, called *Self Not Whole,* that was sponsored by Vancouver's Chinese Cultural Centre.

In the early 21st century, Terence Koh, a Beijing-born artist who grew up in Mississauga, Ontario, burst onto the art scene. Koh, whose work is often associated with new gothic art, has used many forms of media that include photography, sculpture, installations and handmade magazines. His solo exhibitions have been featured in Frankfurt, New York City and Zurich, as well as other venues around the world. Koh was one of the first Chinese Canadian artists to embrace social media when he began hosting a chat and performance show on YouTube in 2008. Some of his guests have included art critic and curator Hans Ulrich Obrist, Converse designer Nathan Jobe and provocative pop star Lady Gaga.

The latter half of the 20th century saw the emergence of many talented Chinese Canadian writers who have made significant contributions to Canadian literature. Although there are examples of Chinese Canadian writing from the frontier days, a distinctive body of literature about the Chinese Canadian experience, written in English, didn't develop until the growth of Canadian-born Chinese. Some of these writers were featured in the anthology *Inalienable Rice,* published in 1979, which is a collection of short stories by both Chinese and Japanese Canadians. Others have become award-winning novelists and achieved mainstream recognition.

Evelyn Lau, born in Vancouver in 1971, was one of the first Chinese Canadian writers to achieve nationwide critical and commercial success. Lau had been writing since the age of six and was deeply passionate about her craft, much to the vexation of her demanding immigrant parents who wanted her to pursue medicine. They forbade her from writing, which led Lau to run away from home at 14 and live on the streets of Vancouver. She documented her experiences, which included entering the sex trade to support herself, in the 1989 memoir *Runaway: Diary of a Street Kid.* She has also published many works of poetry, such as *Oedipal Dreams* in 1992, which was nominated for a Governor General Award, making her, at age 21, the youngest nominee in history.

Sky Lee, born in 1952 in Port Alberni, British Columbia, has written several books about Chinese Canadian identity, cultural divides and sexuality. Her 1990 novel, *Disappearing Moon Cafe,* follows four generations of Chinese Canadian women from a family that runs a cafe. The book won the City of Vancouver Book Award and is considered an early breakthrough for Chinese Canadian fiction.

Paul Yee was born in Spalding, Saskatchewan, in 1956, but grew up in Vancouver's Chinatown. He's the author of many books about Chinese history, including several children's books, and is considered one of the foremost experts on Canada's Chinatowns. His 1996 children's novel *Ghost Train* tackles the history of the railroads. Featuring lush paintings by Harvey Chan, the book won a Governor General Award and was adapted into a play in 2001. Yee has also written for older audiences; for example, the historical book *Saltwater City,* which is an examination of the Chinese experience in Vancouver.

One of Canada's most critically acclaimed writers of Chinese heritage is Wayson Choy. Choy was born in 1939 in Vancouver and grew up in Chinatown before moving to Belleville, Ontario, as a youth. At an early age, he discovered he had a passion for reading. He went on to study creative writing at the University of British Columbia, and one of his teachers was Canadian literary icon Carol Shields. While at university, Choy wrote a short story that eventually developed into his first novel, *The Jade Peony.* The story revolves around three siblings growing up in Vancouver's Chinatown during World War II.

Choy was politically active as a young man and participated in many rallies and campaigns against discriminatory regulations. He protested the Asia Pacific Triangle law that denied entry of many Chinese Canadians to the United States because American officials only allowed a small number of Chinese into the country at the time. Choy had argued that he was a Canadian citizen and, therefore, shouldn't fall under a restriction against the Chinese.

Choy moved to Toronto in the late 1960s and began teaching English. When he published *The Jade Peony* in 1995, about 20 years after he first wrote the short story, the novel became a hit among critics and readers. It won Ontario's Trillium Book Award, the City of Vancouver Book Award and spent six months on the *Globe and Mail's* national bestseller list. Choy has also published memoirs about his life in Chinatown as well as a sequel to *The Jade Peony*, entitled *All That Matters,* in 2004.

In 2010, *The Jade Peony* was chosen to be part of CBC's Canada Reads literary festival. I had the pleasure of chatting with Mr. Choy shortly before the festival was set to begin. The following are excerpts from the interview.

Q: Why do you think *The Jade Peony* has received the response it has had?

If it's well written enough, it will prove itself universally as literature, and that might take time to decide whose books have been best written to be best remembered. In my case, I think I have to make clear that *The Jade Peony* came at the right time, at the right moment, when the consciousness of most Canadians was to be accepting of other voices.

But there were pioneer voices before me. For example, Sky Lee's book *[Disappearing Moon Cafe]* and Paul Yee in his writing. There were other writers who were already publishing short stories here and there who had Chinese or Asian names. So I have to say, although my books seem to have made a splash, that splash only happened because their work was already there and I happened to write one that was popular.

Q: Looking back now, what does the *The Jade Peony* mean to you?

I hope I've written something that will last, but the only way to know that is to see if the book builds bridges instead of walls and lets people understand a period in time that seems so different from today. And if that's the case, then I think the book has, has meaning and worth. And that's how I would see it, but I would not say that I was making any breakthrough. I wrote what I knew; I didn't consciously say, "I'm going to write this book and make a difference." I thought I would write this book and help people understand what I grew up in—the world that was mine.

Q: The majority of Chinese living in Canada today came here after the immigration ban was lifted, and they arrived in a much more accepting country. Many may not even be aware of the history of the first Chinese Canadians. Is it important to you that the stories of the early Chinese live on?

You know, I'm waiting for the artists, the writers, the painters, the storytellers, the historians that will tell of the old ways and the past in a new way. I think what we need now is those who will look back and do their research and discover what was really there in human terms, not in terms of statistics, or the facts, and dates and times, so that the people of that past can be brought back to life again.

I think that's beginning to happen, and it's happened in the third and fourth generations who understand that there are gaps…in our colonial history and those who were colonized have not really told their stories completely.

But I will tell you this, I have heard from some teachers when they are teaching *The Jade Peony* that they have some very resistant [Chinese Canadian] students who take the book home—their parents might be told what it's about, or they might read it themselves even—and they protest [against reading] a book like this about these old Chinese people and these peasants.

"We're not like that, why are we reading that book?" So in other words, there's still a class system in certain groups of people that have come over here who want the past buried because they see their own generation as being better and upper class.

Q: Why do you think some Chinese Canadians are reluctant to explore the past?

I think [younger generations] can imagine [the past] because all they have to do is think of their own grandparents' history. But, you see, their grandparents probably taught them, as many of us in Chinatown were taught, to forget the past. It was shameful—we don't need to talk about it.

Nobody seems to understand that the talking about it makes us more human and suggests a kind of courage that would allow the new generation to carry on with a moral understanding of the past backing up anything that threatens their future. Without understanding that past, their future is constantly threatened.

Q: In your lifetime, there's been such a dramatic change in how Chinese people are viewed. Does this ever surprise you?

I think what's amazing to me is my parents would have been amazed. Because they never expected more than [that] I should find work and make a living and live quietly and happily thereafter. The fact that they had an activist son wasn't very comfortable for them, but I'm pleased to say that my father, and eventually my mother, understood the meaning of what I was doing. I don't know what to say about that, other than the world had changed, and when I was ready to speak out, the world was ready to hear. Those two things had to come together.

The late 1990s and the early 21st century saw the continued development of Chinese Canadian writers and their growing reach and success within Canada. Terry Woo, born in Hamilton, Ontario, in 1971, published the novel *Banana Boys* (1999), a coming-of-age story about five young Chinese Canadian men. The book was adapted as a play for the Asian Canadian Theatre Company. Vincent Lam, who was born in the expatriate Chinese community in Vietnam before immigrating to Canada with his family, became a medical doctor. He wrote *Bloodletting & Miraculous Cures* (2006), a collection of short stories based on some of his experiences in medical school, to wide critical and public acclaim. This book won the prestigious Scotiabank Giller Prize and has since been adapted into an HBO mini-series.

Chinese Canadians have also enriched the field of journalism. Adrienne Clarkson, who immigrated to

Canada with her family from Hong Kong during World War II as refugees, became an investigative reporter and television personality for the CBC. Following her retirement from full-time journalism, she served as Ontario's agent-general in Paris during the 1980s. In 1999, Clarkson was sworn in as Canada's 26th Governor General, the first visible minority and only the second woman to have this honour. She also published books—a biography about Canadian medical legend Norman Bethune, and her bestselling memoir, *Heart Matters* (2006).

Jan Wong, a third-generation Canadian and former Beijing correspondent and columnist for the *Globe and Mail*, has written several critically lauded books. *Red China Blues: My Long March from Mao to Now* (1997) chronicles Wong's time as a young Maoist going to China to witness the Communist transformation. Her enthusiasm for communism, however, largely faded after she witnessed the harsh conditions under which people lived. The book contains a stirring account of the Tiananmen Square crackdown in 1989.

Wong published a follow-up book, *Beijing Confidential* in 2007, which is a memoir of her return to China to track down a young Chinese student whom Wong had reported to authorities during her Maoist years after the student asked Wong to help her emigrate to North America.

Other Chinese Canadian journalists who emerged into the national spotlight during the early 21st century included CBC foreign correspondent Melissa Fung, television personality Wei Chen and Discovery Channel host Ziya Tong.

CHAPTER FIFTEEN

POLITICS

As we've examined in earlier chapters, the Chinese communities in Canada have always been politically and socially active. The early immigrants in Chinatown formed a variety of community organizations, from Freemason groups to the various benevolent associations that provided services and assistance. Throughout China's tumultuous civil war, political groups popped up supporting both opposing sides, and during World War II, Chinese communities across Canada chipped in to raise money for the war effort.

Up until World War II, most forms of politics and activism took place within the Chinese community and not the wider Canadian society. Chinese Canadians didn't have the vote or citizenship and were mostly disengaged (or were prevented from engaging) from Canadian politics at the provincial and federal levels. There were certainly national campaigns and movements to protest discriminatory polices, such as the head tax and the Immigration Act in 1923, but the sphere of political influence was mostly limited to Chinatown. However, this began to change in the post-war years as immigration increased and a new generation of middle-class Chinese emerged in Canada.

The first Canadian of Chinese origin to be elected to the House of Commons was Douglas Jung, in 1957. Jung was born in Victoria in 1925 and enlisted in the Canadian Army during World War II. He was one of the few Chinese Canadians selected for the Special Operations Executive, the spy team trained to infiltrate Japanese-occupied territories in the Pacific.

Following the war, Veterans Affairs Canada provided funds to some soldiers so they could attend university. Jung took advantage of this opportunity and studied at the University of British Columbia and eventually became a lawyer. He made history by becoming the first Chinese Canadian lawyer to be called to the bar, in 1954.

Jung joined the Progressive Conservative Party in the early 1950s, partly because he was so offended by the Liberal Party's discriminatory policies in the past. If you recall, it was the Liberals, under William Lyon Mackenzie King, that passed the Chinese Immigration Act banning almost all Chinese immigration for more than two decades. Jung was elected the Vancouver Centre MP in 1957 and helped bring Chinese Canadian issues to national attention. One of his best-known accomplishments was spearheading an amnesty program during the early 1960s for illegal Chinese immigrants who had come to Canada to reunite with their families using false documents to circumvent the very restrictive immigration policies in effect at the time.

Jung's efforts led policymakers to re-examine the regulations regarding family reunification. During his career, Jung worked with Canadian war veterans groups and cultural organizations such as the Vancouver Symphony. He was named to the Order of Canada in 1990. Jung passed away in 2002 after struggling with a heart condition. In 2007, a federal building in Vancouver was named after him in recognition of his achievements. Jung was the first Chinese face to enter federal politics in Canada, but his groundbreaking career was quickly followed by new politicians.

Arthur Lee, who was born in Alberta but ended up practising law in British Columbia, became the first Chinese Canadian Liberal MP, in 1974. A few years later, he assumed leadership of British Columbia's Liberal Party and became the first Chinese Canadian to lead a provincial party.

During the 1980s and 1990s, several Chinese Canadians followed Jung's and Lee's footsteps in the House of Commons. Raymond Chan and Sophia Leung, both from British Columbia, represented the Liberal Party, and their respective constituents re-elected them multiple times.

Inky Mark (Manitoba) and Michael Chong (Ontario) won seats in the House in the late 1990s and were also re-elected several times.

In 2006, former Toronto City Councillor Olivia Chow was elected as an MP for the NDP and later served as the party's Citizenship and Immigration Critic.

Meili Faille, born in 1972 in Montréal to a Chinese mother and a French Canadian father, became a Bloc Québecois MP in 2004 and was appointed as shadow minister of Citizenship and Immigration by the party.

Many Chinese Canadians received prominent appointments in the latter half of the 20th century. Three Chinese Canadians served as provincial lieutenant-governors during this period of time: David Lam was named British Columbia's provincial governor in 1988, Normie Kwong was named Alberta's in 2005, and Philip Lee was appointed Manitoba's in 2009.

Chinese Canadians also found political success municipally as many have served as mayors. Peter Wing was born in Kamloops, British Columba, in 1914 and made history in 1966 when he became the first Canadian mayor of Chinese origin. He served three mayoral terms in Kamloops. Peter Wong, who was born in Moose Jaw, Saskatchewan, in 1931, later became the mayor of Sudbury, Ontario. He served from 1982 to 1991. Alan Lowe, born in Victoria in 1961, served as the city's mayor between 1999 and 2008.

Chinese immigrants who arrived in Canada in the late 1990s and 2000s are increasingly becoming involved in mainstream politics. In 2007, a number of recent Chinese immigrants, many from mainland China, set up the country's first political party composed mostly of Chinese Canadians. The National Alliance Party was established in Vancouver with the specific mandate of "better living and working conditions for immigrants, and raising the profile of all Chinese living overseas."

FIGHTING FOR RIGHTS

It's important to understand that although Canada's mainstream institutions long ignored Chinese Canadian issues, and Chinese Canadians were shut out of the political discourse for many years, there were always Chinese activists working hard the entire time trying to effect change. During the 20th century, the Chinese community in Canada became increasingly vocal about social equality and rallied together on issues of discrimination.

For several years, Chinese Canadian groups had been calling for further changes to the country's immigration policy, which continued to limit the immigration of people from Asian countries in general. As a result of this situation, overseas Chinese were coming into Canada by using forged documents. It was during this time that Chinese Canadian MP Douglas Jung introduced a motion to help naturalize these illegal immigrants. Finally, in 1967, the federal government overhauled its immigration policy to include a universal point system that didn't discriminate against prospective immigrants because of their ethnicity or place of origin. Chinese immigrants (mostly from Hong Kong but also from Vietnam and Jamaica) began arriving in large numbers.

In 1984, the Chinese Canadian National Council (CCNC) launched a national campaign to collect redress payments from the federal government because of the head tax. The council organized community meetings, produced research materials and generated publicity for the cause.

On June 22, 2006, decades after the CCNC launched their campaign, Conservative Prime Minister Stephen Harper stood up in the House of Commons and apologized to Chinese Canadians affected by the head tax and immigration ban. The federal government also promised to make redress payments of about $20,000 to survivors from that era who had paid the head tax.

Chinese Canadians also came together to promote rights for Chinese overseas. In 1989, following the

Tiananmen Square massacre, Chinese Canadian communities across Canada held rallies calling on governments and human rights groups to respond. In Toronto, more than 30,000 people gathered outside city hall, making it the largest rally in the city's history for an international event. During this time, the federal government relaxed immigration laws for students from mainland China so they could quickly attain Canadian citizenship.

Conclusion

Throughout the course of my research for this book, I came across the stories of many incredible Chinese Canadians. From Won Alexander Cumyow, the first Canadian-born Chinese, to activist and Chinatown hero Jean Lumb, I read their inspirational words and illuminating missives and gleaned much wisdom from their insights. Some of those testimonies have made their way into this book. But I keep thinking back to one particular statement that I believe says a lot about the Chinese people and about Canada. The words are Dr. Henry Fok's, from a speech delivered at the grand opening of the Calgary Chinese Cultural Centre in 1992:

> The Chinese have an expression: "Like the sea being a gathering place of hundreds of rivers regardless of their

sources, broadmindedness commands immense tolerance to different ideas and thoughts regardless of their origin." The primary reason for an outstanding culture to be able to endure thousands of years without losing its vitality is due to its ability to incorporate different ideas and philosophies from other cultures into its own.

Dr. Fok was obviously describing the Chinese culture. But he could very well have been talking about Canada.

Canada is still a young country. But in its short time, it has achieved a great deal. Canadians are viewed internationally as a tolerant, generous society. We've invented many great things, from the telephone, to insulin, to the retractable beer carton handle. So many of the world's finest athletes, entertainers, thinkers, artists and visionaries proudly call Canada their home. Our country's natural beauty and resources are envied throughout the world. But the single best thing about Canada, in my humble opinion, is that our country's greatest successes have yet to come.

The potential of Canadians to do amazing things has no limits. And as this country continues to grow and prosper, its greatest strength will be its diversity. This cultural tapestry that we've woven together is the reason why Canada will be able to endure without losing its vitality. It's our shared wealth of experiences, perspectives and beliefs that help us innovate, progress and overcome new challenges.

We don't live in a perfect society—our tapestry has some tears and loose threads. In a country as ethnically, geographically and socially diverse as Canada is, there are bound to be tensions, misunderstandings and competing interests. True equality is an ideal we have yet to attain.

And though we may never get there, I'm convinced we are heading in the right direction. The evidence can be seen in these pages.

The first Chinese came to Canada because they were good at building things. Many Chinese took the opportunity to escape an impoverished, war-torn China hoping to make a better life. They cut through our thick forests to create roads for wagons. They hammered down rail spikes and helped unite our young country by laying down a railway that stretches coast to coast. But the most important, and lasting, thing those early Chinese in Canada worked so hard to build wasn't a road or a railway. It wasn't even something physically real. They built a bridge to understanding.

The Chinese were considered outsiders from a backward culture, fit for nothing else except the menial work few other Canadians were willing to do. They were treated with hostility, forced to live in ghettos and told they would never belong here—never be "real Canadians."

It got so bad that some Chinese returned to China, thinking that their life in this country would never change. But the Chinese who stayed in Canada were optimistic. They believed that if they worked hard, if they persevered, if they lived like good citizens—even when citizenship was denied to them—then Canadians would someday understand. They'd understand that the Chinese didn't come to Canada to take parts of the country and claim it as their own. The Chinese came here to become part of the country and call it their home, just like everyone else before them.

Eventually Canada did understand. It's because of the sacrifices and efforts of the early Chinese in this country that subsequent generations of Chinese—and people of all other cultures as well—were able to gain acceptance and be considered real Canadians.

Rome wasn't built in a day, and neither will the inclusive "just society" we aspire to have. But that's OK. Because Canada has a lot of people who are good at building things.

Appendix I

Important Events in Chinese Canadian History: A Timeline

1788

John Meares, a British merchant who had been trading in Macau, decides to set up a trading post in (what is now) British Columbia. He enlists about 50 Chinese craftsmen to join him on his voyage to North America. They land on the shores of Nootka Sound, Vancouver Island, marking the first known time a Chinese person steps onto Canadian soil.

1858

Gold is discovered along the Fraser River, leading thousands of Chinese workers to travel north from California. Most gold diggers come through Victoria, at the time one of the busiest port cities in (what is now) Canada. (The Colony of Vancouver Island, founded in 1849, is still separate from the Colony of British Columbia, established in 1858; they will merge in 1866 and join Canada in 1871.) Some early Chinese immigrants establish Canada's first Chinatown in Victoria. Although details from this era are sketchy, it's estimated between 1700 and 4000 Chinese arrive in the country by 1860.

1860

Mrs. Lee, wife of an influential merchant in Victoria, British Columbia, becomes the first Chinese woman to immigrate to (what is now) Canada. Soon after Lee's historic arrival, Won Ling Sing and Wong Shee, a Chinese husband and wife, come to Victoria via San Francisco.

Also in this year, as anti-Chinese sentiment builds, the Colony of Vancouver Island tries to pass a head tax of $10 on Chinese immigrants. The motion is defeated because many politicians anticipate the courts will find the measure too discriminatory to be justified.

1861

Wong Shee gives birth to a boy named Won Alexander Cumyow, thought to be the first Chinese born in (what is now) Canada. He will grow up to be an activist and community leader.

1875

The British Columbia legislature successfully passes a bill that bans Chinese people from voting in provincial elections.

1881

Construction of the Canadian Pacific Railway begins in earnest after years of setbacks. It becomes immediately clear to head contractor Andrew Onderdonk that building the railway will require more manpower than Canada possesses. He hires thousands of Chinese labourers, for about $1 per day, to lay down rail, clear paths through forests and tunnel through mountains. The construction of the railway takes many Chinese away from British Columbia and into other parts of the country, where they will eventually settle.

1885

The national railway is completed. Between the beginning of construction and the completion of the railway, an estimated 16,000 Chinese work on it. There is a big celebratory ceremony as the last spike is driven into the ground in Craigellachie, British Columbia. Not a single Chinese worker is invited.

The same year, the federal government introduces a head tax of $50, imposed upon every person of Chinese origin entering the country, with the exception of some wealthy merchants and temporary visitors such as students or clergymen.

1900–03

Despite the imposition of the head tax, Chinese immigration to Canada continues to grow. Between 1886 and 1894, more than 12,000 Chinese paid the tax and registration fees. The federal government introduces the Chinese Immigration Act and raises the head tax to $100. Three years later, the tax is increased again to a staggering $500. Immigration slows after 1903, but 40,000 Chinese end up paying the head tax between 1904 and 1924. The federal government also introduces the Dominion Election Act, which states that "no woman, idiot, lunatic or criminal shall vote." Visible minorities already excluded from voting provincially are also barred from voting in federal elections.

1907

After an anti-Asian league holds a demonstration in Vancouver, thousands of white Canadians storm into the city's Chinese and Japanese communities. Store windows are broken and signs are smashed. The police declare martial law. Chinese and Japanese residents buy up firearms the next day. No further rioting happens.

World War I (1914–18)

Many Chinese Canadians try to enlist in the military, although Alberta and Ontario are the only provinces to allow Chinese to join. After the war, one dozen Chinese Canadian soldiers are given the right to vote.

1923

The Liberal government, led by William Lyon Mackenzie King, bans all Chinese immigration, with the exception of a few merchants. Many families hoping to reunite are left separated. The Chinese Immigration Act goes into effect on July 1—Dominion Day (now Canada Day). From this moment forward, the Chinese have another name for this day: Humiliation Day. For many years, storekeepers will close up shops on this day as a mark of protest. The Chinese Canadian population will decrease from 39,587 in 1921, to 34,627 in 1941.

World War II (1939–45)

Hundreds of Chinese Canadians sign up for military service, although discriminatory policies prevent most from being placed into duty until the latter stages of the war. Several Chinese Canadians are selected to be part of special spy missions overseas. More than a dozen Chinese women in Vancouver train in first aid and emergency services and form the remarkable all-Chinese female team known as the Women's Ambulance Corps. Chinatowns across the country raise funds for the war effort and buy millions of dollars in war bonds despite rampant unemployment among Chinese.

1947

Following the conclusion of the World War II, Chinese Canadian veterans are granted the right to vote. But the majority of Chinese in Canada are still not able to do so. Lobby groups, led by many Chinese war veterans, launch a campaign to pressure the federal government into lifting the immigration ban and extending federal voting rights to all Chinese Canadians. The horrors of the Holocaust and the formation of the United Nations make Canadian officials more aware of the discriminatory effect of the Chinese ban. Canada lifts the Chinese Immigration Act and extends federal voting rights to the Chinese. Chinese are allowed to work in professional fields such as law, pharmacy and politics. Throughout the next decade, many families will be reunited as spouses and children of naturalized Chinese Canadians are allowed in, although immigration remains strict. In most regards, the Chinese are finally being treated like other Canadian citizens.

1948

The racial exclusion provisions in the Dominion Election Act are officially stripped away. Although the Chinese gained the vote one year earlier, Japanese Canadians finally gain full rights.

Larry Kwong, from Vernon, British Columbia, becomes the first Chinese Canadian to play in the NHL. He suits up for the New York Rangers against the Montréal Canadiens on March 13. His NHL career lasts exactly one game, but his historic appearance on the ice precedes the debut of Willie O'Ree, the first black player in the NHL, by a decade. This same year, Norman Kwong (no relation), from Calgary, becomes the first Chinese Canadian to play in the CFL.

1949

The government in British Columbia allows Chinese Canadians to vote in provincial elections.

1955

Margaret Gee, who grew up in Vancouver's Chinatown, becomes the first female Chinese Canadian lawyer to be called to the bar.

1957

Douglas Jung, a war veteran and lawyer from Vancouver, becomes the first Chinese Canadian elected as a Member of Parliament. Jung runs as a Progressive Conservative, having vowed long ago to never join the Liberal party for its role in instituting the Chinese immigration ban.

1960s

Toronto activist Jean Lumb spearheads the "Save Chinatown" campaign after developers and city officials want to demolish what's left of the city's original Chinatown. Lumb will later receive the Order of Canada because of her efforts.

1966

Peter Wing of Kamloops, British Columbia, becomes the first Chinese Canadian mayor in history. He goes on to serve three mayoral terms in Kamloops.

1967

For several years, Chinese Canadian groups have been calling for further changes to the country's immigration policy, which continued limiting immigration from Asian countries in general. As a result, overseas Chinese have been sneaking into Canada using forged documents. Finally, in 1967, the federal government overhauls its immigration policy to include a universal point system that doesn't discriminate against prospective immigrants because of their ethnicity or place of origin. Chinese immigrants (mostly from Hong Kong but also from Vietnam and Jamaica) begin arriving in large numbers.

1977

The CTV network airs a documentary called "Campus Giveaway" that portrays Chinese Canadian students in an unfair, negative light. It suggests that foreign students are taking over Canadian universities and taking away education opportunities from white students. Mass protests around the country from the Chinese community lead to the formation of the Chinese Canadian National Council, an important organization for drawing attention to discrimination. CTV later apologizes for airing the piece and admits the information presented was inaccurate.

1984

The Chinese Canadian National Council launches a national campaign to collect redress payments from the federal government because of the head tax. The council organizes community meetings, produces research materials and generates publicity for the cause. Despite meeting with federal officials over the next 20 years, no offer of redress is made until 2006.

1989

Chinese Canadian communities across the country hold rallies after the Tiananmen Square massacre, calling on governments and human rights groups to respond. In Toronto, more than 30,000 people gather outside city hall, making it the largest rally in the city's history for an international event. During this time, the federal government allows students from mainland China to apply for Canadian citizenship.

1994

The impending return of Hong Kong to China has fuelled a spike in Chinese immigration to Canada during the past two decades. With the handover three years away, immigration from Hong Kong peaks at 44,000 this year. The federal government decides to end negotiations on head tax redress.

1995

Carole Bell, deputy mayor of Markham, Ontario, complains to the press that "everything's going Chinese" when asked about the proliferation of Chinese mega malls and neighbourhoods in the city. Bell says the influx of Chinese is alienating Caucasian residents and driving them away. Her comments spark a huge uproar across the country. More than 8000 people sign a petition demanding an apology. Shortly after the incident, the

Chinese Canadian National Council organizes a forum on urban planning to bring together developers, investors and city planners to exchange ideas about the challenges of building diverse neighbourhoods.

1997

Hong Kong returns to China after about a century of British rule. Mainland China overtakes Hong Kong as the largest source of Chinese immigration to Canada.

1998

Vivienne Poy, a Hong Kong–born fashion designer, entrepreneur and sister-in-law of Adrienne Clarkson, becomes the first Chinese Canadian senator in history. She is a highly educated individual who often draws attention to Chinese Canadian history during her speeches to the senate and at public functions. In one of her first addresses to the senate, Poy acknowledges that multiculturalism is very much still a work in progress and that education is the key to achieving inclusivity and understanding.

1999

Journalist Adrienne Clarkson becomes Canada's 26th Governor General. She is the first person of Chinese heritage to be appointed to the role and the second woman. She uses this position to promote Canadian culture around the world.

2006

More than 20 years after the Chinese Canadian National Council's campaign began (and several decades after protests from early Chinese Canadians), Conservative Prime Minister Stephen Harper apologizes to Chinese Canadians affected by the head tax and immigration ban. The government also offers redress payments of about $20,000 to survivors from that era who had paid the head tax.

Appendix II

The Chinese Population in Canada

Year	Total	Percent born in Canada	Percent foreign born
1881	4383	< 1	> 99
1891	9129	< 1	> 99
1901	17,312	N/A	N/A
1911	27,831	3	97
1921	39,587	7	93
1931	46,519	12	88
1941	34,627	20	80
1951	32,528	31	69
1961	58,197	40	60
1971	118,197	38	62
1981	289,245	25	75
1991	633,933	27	73
2001	1,029,395	25	75
2006	1,216,600	25	75

Numbers in this chart were taken from census research conducted by The Dominion Bureau of Statistics and Statistics Canada.

Notes on Sources

Bourdain, Anthony. *No Reservations: Around the World on an Empty Stomach*. New York City, NY: Bloomsbury, 2007.

Chinese Canadian National Council. "History." 1997. Chinese Canadian National Council. November 1, 2009. http://www.ccnc.ca/toronto/history

Chinese Canadian Writers Workshop. *Inalienable Rice: A Chinese & Japanese Canadian Anthology*. Vancouver, BC: Powell Street Revue: Chinese Canadian Writers Workshop, 1979.

Chong, Willie. "Force 136." Burma Star Association. November 10, 2009. http://www.burmastar.org.uk/willy_chong.htm

Chow, Jenny. Interview with CBC Radio. July 9, 1958.

Choy, Wayson. Personal interview. February 3, 2010.

Corliss, Richard, Kate Drake, Joyce Huang and Stephen Short. "Cantopop Kingdom." *Time*. September 15, 2001. http://www.time.com/time/magazine/article/0,9171,1000778,00.html

Davis, Chuck. *The History of Metropolitan Vancouver*. Vancouver, BC: Harbour Publishing, 2009.

Dawson, J. Brian. *Moon Cakes in Gold Mountain: From China to the Canadian Plains*. Calgary, AB: Detselig Enterprises, 1991.

Eade, Ron. "T&T Arrives with a Bang." *The Ottawa Citizen*. October 2, 2009.

Harper, Stephen. "PM Addresses Head Tax and Lauds Accomplishments of Chinese Canadians." October 10, 2006. Office of the Prime Minister. http://pm.gc.ca/eng/media.asp?id=1353

Hoe, Ban Seng. *Enduring Hardship: The Chinese Laundry in Canada.* Gatineau, QC: Canadian Museum of Civilization, 2003.

Hooker, Richard. "Ch'ing China: The Opium Wars." 1996. Washington State University. http://www.wsu.edu:8001/~dee/CHING/OPIUM.HTM

Hume, Fred. "Quene Yip: UBC's First Chinese-Canadian Sports Star." February 2008. *The Point.* http://www.intramurals.ubc.ca/thepoint/pdfs/180610.pdf

Ibbitson, John. "For Harper, the future is Asian." *Globe and Mail.* December 7, 2009. http://www.theglobeandmail.com/news/politics/for-harper-canadas-future-is-asian/article1390903/

Knox, Roger. "A Standing Ovation for Trailblazer." *Vernon Morning Star.* April 3, 2009.

Kwong, Norman. Personal interview. February 8, 2010.

Lai, David. *Chinatowns: Towns Within Cities in Canada.* Vancouver, BC: University of British Columbia Press, 1988.

Li, Huai-min. *Portraits of a Challenge: An Illustrated History of the Chinese Canadians.* Toronto, ON: Council of Chinese Canadians in Ontario, 1984.

Li, Peter S. *The Chinese in Canada*. Toronto, ON: Oxford University Press, 1998.

——. "Chinese." *Encyclopedia of Canada's Peoples*. Toronto, ON: Multicultural History Society of Ontario, 1999.

——. "The Rise and Fall of Chinese Immigration to Canada: Newcomers from Hong Kong and Mainland China, 1980–2000." Paper presented to the Conference on Sub-ethnicity in the Chinese Diaspora. September 12–13, 2003. University of Toronto, 2003.

Lindsay, Colin. "The Chinese Community in Canada." Ottawa, ON: Statistics Canada, 2001.

Liu, Melinda. "Kung Fu Fighting for Fans." *Newsweek*. August 23, 2008. http://blog.newsweek.com/blogs/beijingolympics/archive/2008/08/23/kung-fu-fighting-for-respect.aspx

MacKay, Donald. *The Asian Dream: The Pacific Rim and Canada's National Railway*. Vancouver, BC: Douglas & McIntyre, 1986.

Myles, Stephanie. "Canada and the UFC: A match made in Montreal." *Vancouver Sun*. April 18, 2009. http://www.vancouversun.com/sports/MMA/Canada+match+made+Montreal/1511395/story.html

Oakland Museum of California. "Chinese Man." 1998. Oakland Museum of California. http://museumca.org/goldrush/silver-chman.html

Osborne, Jari. *Unwanted Soldiers*. National Film Board of Canada, 1999. http://www.nfb.ca/film/Unwanted_ Soldiers

Parkinson, Rhonda. "The Ubiquitous Cup of Tea— Chinese Tea Drinking." About.com. http://chinesefood. about.com/od/chineseteaandliquor/a/chinesetea.htm

Poy, Vivienne. "History of the Chinese in Canada." Ottawa, ON: Senate, 36th Parliament. February 2, 1999.

Pratt, Sir John T. *China and Britain*. Northampton, England: Clarke and Sherwell, 1965.

Roberts, J.A.G. *China to Chinatown: Chinese Food in the West*. London, England: Reakton Books, 2002.

Scrivener, Leslie. "Marshalling Praise for Art of Tai Chi." *Toronto Star*. September 9, 2007. http://www.thestar. com/News/article/254609

Soon, Chad. "The Return of King Kwong." *Insider's Edge*. November/December 2009.

Stainsby, Mia. "Emerging tea sommeliers hitting the right notes." Canwest News Service. October 14, 2009. http://www.vancouversun.com/life/eat-drink/becomes +trendy+industry+turns+over+leaf/2513239/Emerging +sommeliers+hitting+right+notes/2100835/story.html

Trumbull, Robert. "Hong Kong Holds Life of Contrasts: Rich and Poor, Good and Bad All Exist Side by Side." July 9, 1961. *The New York Times*. http://www.nytimes.com/specials/hongkong/ archive/610709hk.html

Tsang, Steve. *A Modern History of Hong Kong: 1841–1997.* London, England: I.B. Tauris & Co. Ltd., 2003.

Unschuld, Paul Ulrich. *Medicine in China: A History of Ideas.* Berkeley, CA: University of California Press, 1985.

Veteran Affairs Canada. "Heroes Remember—Canadian Chinese Veterans." November 20 2007. http://www.vac-acc.gc.ca/remembers/sub.cfm?source=collections/hr_cdnchinese

Wang, Shuguang and Lucia Lo. "Chinese Immigrants in Canada: Their Changing Composition and Economic Performance." Paper presented to the Conference on Sub-ethnicity in the Chinese Diaspora. September 12–13, 2003. University of Toronto, 2003.

Wong, Marjorie. *The Dragon and the Maple Leaf: Chinese Canadians in World War II.* London, England: Pirie Publications, 1994.

Yee, Paul. *Chinatown: An Illustrated History of the Chinese Communities of Victoria, Vancouver, Calgary, Winnipeg, Toronto, Ottawa, Montréal and Halifax.* Toronto, ON: James Lorimer & Co., 2005.

ADRIAN MA

Adrian Ma has worked for the *Toronto Star* and the CBC and has written for a variety of newspapers and magazines, including the *Hamilton Magazine,* the *Echo Weekly, YA Magazine* and the *Waterloo Chronicle.* He has a Masters degree in Journalism from Ryerson University in Toronto and an Honours BA in Philosophy and Political Science from Wilfrid Laurier University.

Adrian won a Canadian Community Newspapers Association award for Best Campus News Story while attending Laurier. He also received a fellowship from the Canadian Association of Journalists in 2009 to travel to Hong Kong to produce a feature about the city's counterculture.